Baby
monthly

Inside your baby's mind – from birth to one year

Carol Pope

BBC Books

To my husband Peter and my parents whose support never flags

Published by BBC Books,
a division of BBC Enterprises Limited,
Woodlands, 80 Wood Lane
London W12 OTT

First Published 1994
© Carol Pope 1994
ISBN 0 563 37070 X

Designed by Isobel Gillan
Set in Bembo
Printed and bound in Great Britain by Clays Ltd, St Ives plc
Cover printed by Clays Ltd, St Ives plc

Contents

ACKNOWLEDGEMENTS

A book like this cannot be compiled alone. It calls on the knowledge and expertise of many people. I would like to thank those who have generously given of their patience and time to talk about their work, check manuscripts and generally make their brains available for picking. Particular thanks are due to Dr Peter Willatts who has been unstintingly helpful; to John Oates, Dr Howard Steele, Professor Colwyn Trevarthen, Professor George Butterworth, Dr Vasudevi Reddy, Professor Karen Wynn, Dr Suzanne Zeedyk, Dr Ian St James Roberts, Dr Ronald Barr, Dr Gillian Harris, Professor Lynne Murray, Professor Giannis Kugiumutzakis, Dr Alan Slater, Professor Kevin Connolly, Professor Michael Tomasello, Professor Edward Melhuish, Professor Michael Howe.

Thanks are also specially due to Edward Goldwyn and television production company Goldwyn Associates, for all their help and co-operation.

PICTURE CREDITS

BBC Books would like to thank the following for providing photographs and for permission to reproduce copyright material. While every effort has been made to trace and acknowledge all copyright holders, we would like to apologize should there have been any errors or omissions.

Renée Baillargeon, University of Illinois at Urbana–Champaign page 114; **Barnaby's Picture Library** pages 50 (R. Rodway) and 131 (L. Howling); **Bubbles** pages 6 (J. Farrow), 93,166,194,199,215,235, (all L.J. Thurston) and 247 (F. Rombout); **Elizabeth Crews** page 151; **Jennifer Fry** page 48; **Goldwyn Associates** pages 14 and 80; **Sally and Richard Greenhill** pages 21,203,and 210; **Robert Harding** (Explorer/Negré) page 55; **Harlow Primate Laboratory, University of Wisconsin** page 201; **Anita Huges** page 190; **Camilla Jessel** pages 9,27,95,107,170,172,179,180,220,and 230;**Reflections** (Jennie Woodcock) pages 16,77,110,128,138 (right),156,192and 225; **Alan Slater, University of Exeter** pages 36 and 134; **Peter Willatts, University of Dundee** page 138 (left); **Karen Wynn, University of Arizona** page 112.

All remaining photographs were taken for the BBC by **Camilla Jessel**.

Introduction

The core of the TV series *Baby Monthly,* is the research that has revealed the astonishing things babies do. It details the important parts of the complex dance they perform with their parents which develops them into both talking and thinking members of the human race. What is unexpected in this new picture is how purposefully the babies lead in this intimate partnership – right from the moment of birth.

Parents react intuitively to their babies but knowing what the scientists have discovered will add enormously to the pleasure of being with their babies, and to an understanding of the importance of what is going on at particular moments. The range of the science is too broad for the TV series to do it full justice but it is wonderfully explored and developed in this book.

Edward Goldwyn
Executive Producer *Baby Monthly*

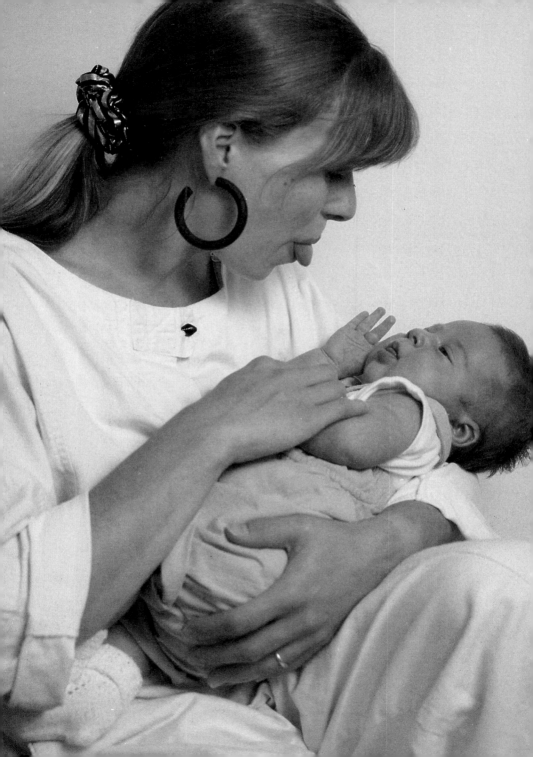

CHAPTER 1

Primed for Life

Jacob opened his eyes almost tentatively. Only minutes before he was curled up, snug, comfortable and secure in a darkened womb. Above him, his mother bent her face over his. The baby's gaze wavered, watched, wavered. 'Hallo,' she said. 'And welcome to the world.' Then slowly and very deliberately she opened her mouth wide and stuck out her tongue. The baby's eyes stayed open. She held the pose. He watched. Her tongue strained right out. Thirty seconds passed, nothing happened. His eyes remained fixed on her face. What was going on behind them? Then his mouth twitched, twitched again, and slowly opened. She watched this time in excitement bordering on disbelief as he paused and, with an uncertain stabbing movement, stuck out his tongue. At fifteen minutes old, he had imitated his mother.

The newborn baby's ability to imitate is so unexpected, so difficult to explain that psychologists for twenty years have argued over whether or not it really happens for twenty years. To accept that newborn babies can copy others you have to credit them with a lot

The newborn's ability to imitate is so difficult to explain that psychologists have argued about it for twenty years.

more at birth than had been traditionally thought. Instead of the empty bucket theory – that new babies are little more than vessels waiting to be filled – researchers have been gradually pushed towards the view that, even at birth, babies are capable of some extraordinarily sophisticated skills. The problem has been mostly one of accessing them. How can you get inside a baby's head and find out what is going on in there? Also if you are watching the behaviour of young babies who are still learning to control their bodies, how do you know which responses are meant and which are at random? This has been the biggest problem in convincing scientists that newborn babies are imitating the faces they see rather than just randomly making the same expressions.

There now seems little doubt that many very young babies can, and do, imitate facial expressions, sticking out their tongues, opening their mouths wide and pursing their lips 'bimbo' style. Some have even been shown to match happy, sad and surprised expressions when only two or three days old.

It seems an extraordinary thing that these infants, who have only recently opened their eyes for the first time, should be able first of all to recognize an expression on another face and secondly to transfer that expression in some way to their own features, and it is not just facial expressions they can copy. Some babies will open and close their fists in imitation and copy an adult saying 'ah, ah'. Does this mean babies are born with some idea that they have eyes, a mouth, tongue, hands... equivalent to what they are seeing out there? Or is imitation just some form of reflex?

Professor Giannis Kugiumutzakis is one of a handful of psychologists throughout the world who have been studying this imitation marvel for years. Working from his laboratory on the Greek island of Crete, close to the delivery room in a Heraklion hospital, he regularly examines babies only minutes after their birth.

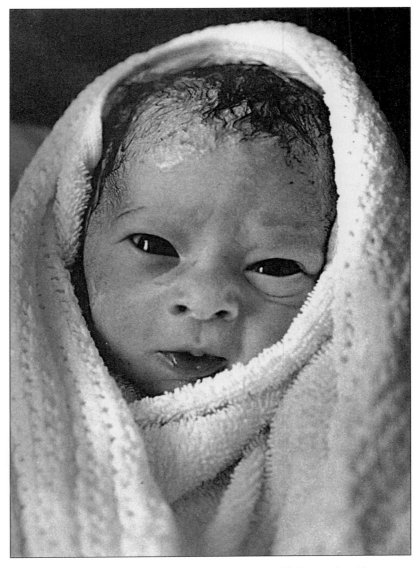

Primed for life — newborns arrive in the world alert and with all systems raring to go.

Often he is actually present at the delivery. Getting permission from parents poses few problems on the island – out of nearly 500 pairs of parents, Professor Kugiumutzakis claims only two have turned him down.

'Greek people are very open,' he said. 'In Sweden where I also worked we had to pay parents to come to the laboratory. Here they are so happy after their child has been born, some of them try to give me money! Of course I always refuse, but sometimes as a present I give them a copy of the experimental episode.'

From his work Kugiumutzakis is convinced that this early imitation is no reflex.

'If it was... you would expect all the babies to react, but we have non-imitators... and you would expect stereotypical movements but we have huge individual variation.'

He sees imitation as the babies' first efforts to communicate, and, more controversially, he believes that this communication is not just about sharing the same kind of movements but about sharing the same kind of emotions.

'We know from other studies,' he said, 'that newborn babies discriminate their own crying from the cry of another newborn baby, and that they cry to the cry of the other newborn baby. They don't cry when they listen to their own tape-recorded crying. They cry only to the tape recording of another newborn baby of the same age... It is a dramatic example of empathy.'

It is Kugiumutzakis's belief that babies not only have a greater range of emotions than they are normally credited with, but that they are ready and willing to share them in a two-way process which actually helps the newborn's brain to develop:

'Immediately after birth we are born with one part of the mind ready for dialogues not with words but with gestures, facial expressions, movements transferring intentions and reading intentions on the part of the mother... It is not something mysterious, it is very simple – the movement is something more than just movement, it transfers mental states.'

This suggestion that early imitation could be the first effort at communication between baby and mother strikes a chord which echoes through current thinking about baby development. Time and again, as we will see, the latest research points to the importance of this early dialogue between the baby and the person closest to him, usually his mother, for many other aspects of development. Could imitation be one of the first sparks to set this communication in motion? Certainly some recent work by psychologist Mikael Heimann in Gothenburg suggests that babies who are strong imitators at birth are likely to have a stronger interaction with their mothers at three months. It is too early to say yet whether this effect carries on into later life, but the first signs are there that good early communication between babies and mothers builds on itself.

To see how these early imitation sessions could set the dialogue pendulum in motion we follow the research path to Edinburgh where one of the world's leading child psychologists Professor Colwyn Trevarthen has filled in another piece of the jigsaw. One of his team's most exciting findings in the 1970s was that while babies imitate their mothers, it is even more common for the mothers to imitate their babies. When baby makes a face, mum makes a face. When baby makes a sound, mum echoes it. Why should mothers do such a thing? Ask them and many mothers are quite unconscious of even doing it.

'It just seems natural,' is a typical response. Others are aware of what they are doing and trying to do. 'It's like having a kind of conversation but without the words.' 'It's our way of having a little chat.' 'He can't talk to me yet so I guess I'm trying to get into his world and speak his language.'

In other words it is all about communication, and the effect of all
this mutual imitation is, it seems, to strengthen the link between
parents and babies. Certainly later studies have shown that imitation
leads to more eye-to-eye contact which is one sign of a strong bond
between babies and those who care for them. There is also evidence
that the babies of unresponsive mothers do not connect so well. It
seems, then, that mothers and their babies could be primed in some way
to imitate each other as the very earliest form of communication –
before smiling, before vocalization – making a link which is
strengthened by every message that passes along it.

Imitation is just one of the many abilities of newborn babies
which have captured psychologists' attention over recent years. As a
result the psychologists have been forced to dramatically revise the
views held earlier this century that the world of the young baby is,
in William James's words, just a 'blooming, buzzing confusion'. In
lighting the fuse under this myth they have devised some ingenious
methods for tapping into the baby's secret world and finding out
what goes on in there. This has led to all sorts of unexpected discoveries – that babies prefer curved to straight lines, that they have
some early understanding of numbers, that they can remember
songs and poems they heard in the womb – discoveries which
suggest not only that the womb is the very earliest of early learning
centres, but also that the baby is born 'pre-programmed' or primed
for life.

To find a window on the baby's inner world, the researchers try
to 'home' in on something under the baby's control – such as sucking,
moving his eyes or turning his head – and use this to tell them
about something else.

Twenty years ago in Edinburgh, Tom Bower was showing that
even very young babies could learn to switch on a light by turning
their heads. Captured on film, the technique today looks rather

crude but the effect is as stunning as ever. The hours-old baby is propped comfortably in a half-lying position so that he can move his head freely. On one side is a light waiting to be lit. Awake and alert, the baby spontaneously moves his head around jerkily. As he turns to the right, the bulb lights up with a buzzing noise. The baby's eyes fix on the bulb. He jerks to the left. Nothing happens. Left again, nothing happens. His head rolls to the right and, bingo, the light is on again. Within minutes the baby is regularly turning his head right to light the bulb. He has solved one of his first-ever problems.

It is through tricks like this that psychologists have tried to find out just what it is like to be a baby. Using the logic that the infant's experience of the world must come through the five senses – hearing, sight, taste, touch and smell – they have started by studying these in newborns. What they have found has thrown a new light not just on the abilities of newborn babies but, more crucially, on the importance of the channel of communication between babies and mothers.

What can newborn babies hear?

The big surprise for many parents is the discovery that babies have been listening in on the world for some time before they are born. Using the way babies suck, psychologist Anthony De Casper has shown that babies already know their mother's voice when they are born. What he did was devise a stunningly simple but ingenious series of experiments giving the babies the chance to choose between listening to their mother's voice or the voice of a stranger. The babies were fitted with headphones through which they could hear a tape either of mum reading a story by Dr Seuss or an unknown woman reading the same passage. The babies could

An ingenious series of experiments using their ability to suck has opened up a window on babies' minds. By allowing them to make choices between different pictures and sounds through changing their rate of sucking psychologists have discovered that babies recognize their mother's voice and face virtually from birth.

switch the voices by changing the way they sucked on a special dummy or pacifier, which was wired up to a computer. By sucking faster or slower the babies could change the tape. Within minutes they discovered that they could control who was talking, and, once they had fathomed out how to do it, they sucked in a way that brought them mum's voice. In other words, when only hours old, the babies knew what their mum's voice sounded like, and, having had only the briefest of chances to meet and get to know mum in the outside world, they were drawn to her voice rather than that of another womans.

Later studies took this finding to even more surprising levels by showing that two-day-old infants can tell their mother's voice from a stranger's on the basis of only one syllable! The tiniest sound-bite is all it takes to tell them: 'That's my mum!'

Another surprise came from an experiment in which De Casper asked pregnant women to sing the nursery rhyme 'Mary Had a Little Lamb' frequently in the fortnight before they expected to give birth. It was the ultimate 'Listen With Mother' experience. After birth the newborn babies were given a choice – through the sucking test – between 'Mary Had a Little Lamb' and another song, both sung by their mothers. The babies voted with their sucks for their old familiar womb song – 'Mary Had a Little Lamb'. Similarly a well publicized study in Belfast captured the public imagination by showing that babies whose mothers watched soap operas such as *Neighbours* when they were pregnant recognized the theme tunes when they were born. Somehow, even before making their entrance into the world, babies listen in, learn and, even more surprisingly, remember what they have heard going on out there.

What babies hear in the womb is a muffled version of outside sounds and chief among those sounds is mum's voice. The actual sound may seem a bit different when they come out into the world but they soon get used to that. Given the choice between a pure and a filtered version of their mother's voice representing how it would sound in the womb, hours-old babies choose the filtered one. This preference, however, soon disappears – usually after the first day or so – by which time they will have heard the real thing and somehow made a decision that is what they should be homing in on.

In fact all the features likely to mark out a mother's voice seem to be particularly attractive to newborn babies. Higher pitch sounds, soft speech and speech patterns, rather than single-note sounds, are

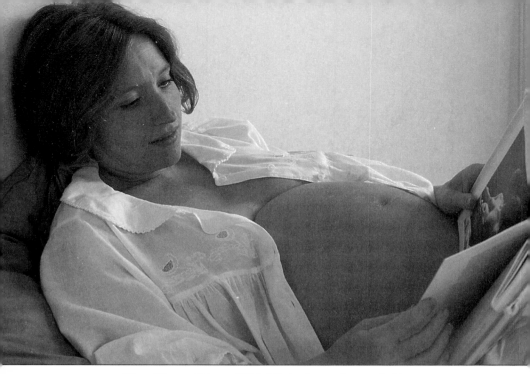

The ultimate 'Listen With Mother' experience – babies get to know their mother's voice while still in the womb.

all on their preferred list. They like women's voices rather than men's but will give a good response to a man who raises the pitch of his voice. Again it looks as if babies are primed from the first to listen to mother.

What can newborn babies smell?

Using the head-turning trick, described earlier, it is quite easy to show that babies of only a few days old can tell their mother's smell. If a breast pad soaked in mum's milk is placed on one side of the head and one with a stranger's milk on the other side, babies tend to turn more towards their mother's pad. There is even evidence that breastfed babies can identify the smell of their mother's sweat. Curiously, the same does not seem to be true of bottle-fed babies. Breastfed babies are more often in close skin contact with their mothers than bottle-fed babies, so have more opportunity to learn that special mother smell. No research appears to have been done on whether bottle-fed babies prefer the smell of teat sterilizing fluid to the smell of their mother's milk, but it would be interesting to know.

So it seems that not only are babies born with a working sense of smell, they are also able to make an association between 'this smell' and something else – this situation? this person? In fact mothers, too, although they may be only dimly conscious of it, can recognize their own babies by their smell, and, interestingly, this seems to be true for new mums whether their deliveries are vaginal or by Caesarean section. Many mothers confess that they find that special warm, milky baby smell, very evocative. As one said: 'It makes me want to bury my nose in that lovely cove between my baby's neck and shoulder'. This sensitivity to each other's smell looks like more evidence for mother and baby being set up with another communication channel.

What can newborn babies taste?

The answer seems to be that they can distinguish all four basic tastes – sweet, salt, sour and bitter. Of course they do not get much opportunity for variety yet but from birth they seem to have a bit of a sweet tooth, preferring sweet tastes to all the rest. Researchers sometimes use drops of a sweet solution as a reward when persuading babies to perform tasks like those that have been described. If, however, the solution they are sucking gets too sweet they stop. It is probably no coincidence that breast milk tastes sweet.

What about the sense of touch?

By measuring heart rate, and using puffs of air, psychologists have established that newborn babies are highly sensitive to touch, especially around the mouth and hands. Whether babies can recognize their mothers by touch – or indeed whether mothers can recognize their own babies by touch – is one of those fascinating questions yet to be answered. The idea of skin-to-skin contact being specially important lies at the heart of the concept of bonding.

Bonding became a 'buzz' word in the 1970s when the idea that the first hours after birth might be specially important for the long-term attachment of babies and mothers landed on a world where many hospitals still whisked babies away shortly after birth and kept them separated from their mothers in off-ward nurseries. Mothers and, for the first time fathers too, were beginning to reclaim some of the childbirth process from the medical world and demand more say in how their babies were born and treated in the first hours and days. The concept of early bonding being important sat well with the popular mood.

It was the work of two American doctors, Klaus and Kennel, which set the fuse burning. They found what they suspected was a worldwide pattern in how mothers acted when their babies were presented to them, naked and newborn. First the mothers touched the baby's fingers or toes, then they stroked the limbs and finally they rubbed the baby's abdomen with a gentle massaging move-ment. The theory went that if this was, as it seemed, something that women everywhere did, then it must be biologically programmed and therefore important to mothers and babies. The analogy was drawn between bonding and imprinting – the process by which geese and other birds automatically follow the first thing they see when they open their eyes. The crux of it was that bonding had to happen in a critical period some time after birth. Skin-to-skin contact between baby and mother was seen as important, and babies – sometimes with the umbilical cord still attached – were placed on to their mothers' chests to help the bonding begin.

Naturally many mums who were not in a position to enjoy this early bonding period – perhaps because their babies were born prematurely and in need of intensive care, perhaps because they themselves were too ill, perhaps because hospital procedures prevented it – felt guilty and worried that their relationships with their babies would be jeopardized. Adoptive parents were also concerned that they could never make up for those lost moments. Later work, though, led to the theory being substantially diluted – especially as far as any critical period is concerned. Study after study has been done to see how that early bonding period affects mothers and babies later.

The studies looked at how much mothers smile, sing, hug, kiss and eyeball their babies over the following weeks and months. Do they do it less if they missed out on that early time? While some studies hint at an extra special relationship in the earliest weeks they have failed again and again to come up with any hard evidence that this continues later. Most professionals readily recognize that the bonding process can take place over a much longer period than was initially suggested.

Clinicians, like Valerie Binney at Sheffield Children's Hospital, a specialist in parent-child relationships, is convinced that the idea of some crucial period has been overplayed. She, and most of her colleagues, believe that people come to attachment slowly and in varying ways. Much more important than that first hour is the relationship the parents had with their parents. The foundations for something as vital as the attachment of mothers and babies are unlikely to be crucially linked to a few minutes after birth – a traumatic event for both. It makes much more sense to think of bonding taking place over a longer time scale. Professionals are now at pains to reassure all mothers that, special though those early moments might be, bonding can be safely put on 'hold'.

This is not to say that the earliest minutes are not very special. Both fathers and mothers can find huge enjoyment and satisfaction in meeting, handling and exploring their baby just after birth. Many parents class these moments as life's highest points.

One set of women for whom that early period can prove particularly helpful in getting the relationship off to a good start is mothers who are expected to have problems in becoming attached to their babies. In these cases it seems the opportunity for early bonding can 'jump start' the attachment process.

What can newborn babies see?

Picture an adult being handed a very sophisticated high-tech camcorder for the first time and you probably have an idea of what it must be like for the baby opening his eyes on the world for the first time. Tracking is jerky and slow, images are out of focus, and sophisticated things like distance and depth of field take a while to develop. If anyone moves their face near the viewfinder this little cameraman automatically tries to 'home' in on them. In addition to all these mechanical controls to be learned, the images themselves – objects, shapes, lines, figures, colours, movement – are new to the baby. What do they mean? How on earth does he begin to sort it all out?

A huge amount of research has gone into answering these questions and, piece by piece, experimenters are building up the jigsaw. They have established for instance that new babies do see but in

Young babies see best close up. Their fuzzy vision probably eliminates the scenery from their world.

an unfocused way which probably eliminates the background scenery from their world. Their best range is about 25-30 centimetres (10-12 inches) — round about the distance at which the mother's face looms when the baby is held in her arms. It is unlikely that babies can see anything at all in the womb so the sense of sight is the one that is really quite raw on birth... and one in which a huge amount of learning takes place in a relatively short time. In fact by six months old a baby's vision is usually sharper than most adults'.

To check out exactly what babies can see, and what they cannot, one trick often used by researchers is known as habituation. When a baby is shown something new — say, a picture of a happy face — he will look at it for a long spell at first, then less and less each time he is shown it. It is as if, after a while, he becomes bored with looking at the same old thing. This is the point at which psychologists say he has become habituated to the stimulus. The experimenters then change the picture – say, to a sad face – and measure how long the baby looks at it this time. If he cannot tell the difference he will not watch it for any longer. If he can, he will spend longer looking at it. This change in looking time, after a change in the stimulus, is called the recovery.

Using this, and similar methods, researchers have found that babies particularly like looking at faces. Even minutes after birth they would rather look at a face-like shape than anything else in the world. In fact it does not seem as if they have much choice in the matter. If a face appears, slowly moving near them, the babies' eyes lock on to it automatically. By stripping down images and watching babies' reactions to elements, such as lines, angles and so on, researchers have discovered that among the cues that attract young babies' eyes are curved lines and slow movement – the sort of cues which would be naturally given by a mother's head as she holds her baby.

Amazingly, within the first few hours of birth, it seems babies know their mother's face. Using the sucking trick, researchers in Texas took babies of only one and two days old and allowed them to choose between looking at a picture of their mother's face or a strange woman's face. The babies sucked for their mother's face even when the stranger was very similar to mum in hair colour, and eyes, hairstyle and complexion. In a similar *Baby Monthly* experiment it took Jacob only twenty seconds to work out that by sucking he was controlling the pictures he saw. He worked harder to see his mother's face and hear her voice saying 'Hallo baby' rather than one of the other *Baby Monthly* mums. How such young babies have already worked out who mum is remains one of the many questions to which psychologists are still seeking an answer.

It seems that even from birth babies are capable of a lot more than most of us imagine. Even as the hours-old baby is feeding he is absorbing much more than milk. He is drinking in information about his environment, and for him that environment is mostly his mum – her voice, her face, her smell... We may not know all the details or the implications yet but what does come across from the research is the importance of communication, even at the very earliest stages. Talking, singing, looking, smiling, touching, holding, feeding – even smelling – seem to offer links through which the rapport between babies and those caring for them can be built, and life's most important dialogue can begin.

Fascinating Findings

Until as recently as 1940 premature babies were exhibited in glass incubators at major world fairs in London, Berlin and the United States. They competed with freak shows and fan dancers to draw in huge crowds of spectators.

Also, until fairly recently, operations were performed on some premature babies without the use of anaesthetic as it was believed they were incapable of feeling pain.

When only twice the size of a jelly-baby, the human foetus can already swallow, suck and grasp. Only fifteen weeks after their origins as a single cell, babies can yawn in the womb.

🎲 The movement of the foetus in the womb appears to be important for its development. Chick embryos prevented from moving by local anaesthetic to the joints were unable to move later after being born because their joints had frozen into bone. Some scientists believe a similar process could be responsible for the fact that babies with alcoholic mothers are sometimes born with cleft palates. They suggest this could be due to the anaesthetic effects of alcohol on the foetus's mouth movements.

🎲 From about six months after conception, babies are already showing a remarkable degree of internal organization. Their womb-bound days are already taking on their own cyclical routine – forty minutes of rest followed by about the same time spent in activity. By the eighth month the foetus can suck his thumb and open his eyes.

🎲 Mother's size is more important than father's in determining the birth weight of babies. This was shown to be true for horses at least, through dramatic experiments crossing tiny Shetland ponies with huge carthorses. The foals, however, grew up to be more or less in between their parents in height.

🎲 Babies born with big tummies are less likely to suffer later from high levels of cholesterol according to a recent study at Southampton University. Researchers there obtained measurements of the abdomens of more than 200 babies born in Sheffield between 1939 and 1940. Following them up as fifty-year-olds, they found that babies with small tummies were more likely to have high cholesterol as adults. The size of a newborn baby's tummy is largely determined by the size of its liver – the organ that breaks down cholesterol.

More evidence is coming to light from research in Scotland and Germany, that breast is best. Mothers' milk, say the scientists, contains fatty acids which are vital to the development of the baby's brain. These – especially substances known as DHA and AA – are not normally included in formula milk so bottle-fed babies may miss out on them altogether. Most of a baby's food in the first six months is taken up by the brain – itself ninety per cent fat – and growing at a tremendous rate at this stage. Failure to thrive in this period can hold up the brain's development, though if caught and addressed, babies can catch up. The richest breast milk is only released towards the end of a feed, so the advice from expert Dieter Wolke in Germany is to completely empty one breast before switching sides.

Could additional fatty acids added to formula milk make babies more intelligent? An experiment being carried out in Dundee could soon have the answer. Milupa, the babyfood manufacturers, are currently testing a new milk formula containing added fatty acids on 1000 babies across Europe. At each centre the babies will be split into three groups – one breastfed, one bottle-fed, and one bottle-fed with added fatty acids. Which group grows the fastest? How well do babies accept the new formula? These are the questions the researchers will be asking, but in Dundee the babies will also be tested on various IQ measures throughout their first year. Will the added fatty acids make a difference to their performance? If the study is a success bottle-feeding mothers could soon be able to give their babies formula milk much closer to breast milk than has been previously available. Another group to benefit will be premature babies who often miss out on breast milk. Donor breast milk has been unavailable in recent years because of the problems of HIV.

What you can do with your baby

Reflexes

Newborn babies show a variety of reflexes, some of which like rooting – searching for the nipple – and sucking, are obviously geared to survival, others less so. The extent, however, to which they show these reflexes varies enormously, not only between individual babies but in the same baby at different times. Factors like the time since the last feed and whether the baby is awake or asleep can be important, and some reflexes, like the walking one (opposite), disappear within a few weeks.

Rooting: gently stroke your baby's cheek towards the mouth. His head will turn to the side that is being touched, as if looking for the nipple. Some babies show this reflex much more strongly than others – even opening their mouths and making sucking movements.

Babinski reflex: gently stroke the outer side of the sole of your baby's foot. The toes usually curl outwards like a fan. It is not clear what use, if any, this reflex might have but lack of it can sometimes be a sign of a neurological disorder.

Stepping out – the walking reflex is still a bit of a mystery. Present at birth, it disappears long before babies are capable of walking properly.

Walking reflex: hold your baby upright, under the arms with his feet on the floor or table. As you move him forward, keep the contact between his feet and the floor. He will take 'steps' – not with both feet at the same time but alternately with each foot. It is as if the co-ordination needed for walking later is somehow pre-programmed in the baby – all he needs is strength and balance and he could be off. This reflex usually disappears within the first couple of months. Why should it disappear long before real walking is a possibility? Could it be that the programme is still in there but the babies' legs simply get too heavy to lift? Researchers attached weights to the legs of four-week-old infants to test this out. Not very surprisingly they stopped stepping... almost completely. Trying the same experiment with the babies' legs underwater, where the pull of the weights is less, the babies continued to step.

Communication

If making the communication link between baby and mother – or father – is as important as it seems from current research then it only seems logical to make the most of it right away. Babies enjoy being talked to in a gentle way, and they like hearing adults humming and singing to them. An early rapport can be started simply by following the direction of your baby's gaze and positioning your face so that he is looking at you. Then smile and say something friendly. It doesn't matter what you say. You could tell him about your family history or the plot of *War and Peace*. At this stage it is the tone rather than the content that he responds to.

To get the imitation response it is important to pick the right moment when your baby is awake and attentive. Take him in your arms and, while he has his eyes open and is looking alert, put your head in his field of vision at a distance of around 24 centimetres (10 inches). Now when you are sure his eyes are on you, open your mouth wide and stick out your tongue in an exaggerated way. Hold the pose, repeat it several times, and watch. There is likely to be a delay of perhaps half-a-minute before he responds.

You can try the same thing with different expressions such as opening your mouth wide, making your mouth open and close – the baby's may well open and close, too – fluttering your eyelashes or saying 'ah'. It is important though to choose something that he would naturally do. Some babies seem to respond better than others and responses may be delayed, fragmentary or fleeting. They may also be hard to detect but when they happen they feel wonderful, to mum and dad at least.

CHAPTER 2

What's going on behind those Eyes ?

Look into the eyes of a four-week-old baby and you can be startled at what you see there. Can babies of a few weeks old really know anything? Can they really think? I vividly remember looking into my son's eyes when he was just one month old and, although it seemed fanciful, what I thought I saw there was wisdom... a sense of some ancient knowledge. I suppose it is what psychologists might describe as innate intelligence. To me, and I suspect to many mothers, it was as convincing as any scientific demonstration that babies are no blank slates just waiting for the world to write on them.

At about the same time, in 1979, two psychologists, Meltzoff and Borton, were coming to a similar conclusion in a much more scientific way. They astonished academic circles with a simple but elegant demonstration which showed that babies' brains work on a much more sophisticated level than most psychologists had guessed. What they did was to prepare two sets of rubber dummies. One had a normal smooth teat, the other was covered in knobbly bumps. Without letting the babies see them, they gave the teats to two groups of four-week-olds. The infants were allowed to suck for a minute or two until they had got the feel of the dummies. Then they were given the choice between looking at two large models of the teats – one knobbly, one smooth. The experimenters stood back and watched. Which model would the babies choose? What they found was that the babies preferred to look at the dummy which matched the one they had been sucking.

Somehow it seemed, at only four weeks old, babies were able to pool information across the senses. They could take the feeling of what they held in their mouths – a knobbly teat – and build from that an image in their minds of what that object should look like. They were then able to match that mental image with the model they saw. It looked as if babies were capable of something much more like real thinking than scientists had imagined possible. Nowhere has that been better explored than through looking at what babies can see.

The visual world of the newborn baby is a shadowy affair. She sees contrast and likes to look at bright colours and dark lines on white but the contrasts are not so stark as they are for adults. Everything has a slightly washed-out look. As we saw in chapter one the baby sees best at around 30 centimetres (10-12 inches) but even then images are slightly fuzzy until the visual system matures. In finding out how babies learn to see, researchers have stripped vision down to its nuts and bolts and presented babies with screen tests of lines, angles, dots and shapes in varying degrees of contrast, colour and brightness.

The gradual discovery over the last few years that babies are born with a highly organized visual system has been a major surprise for researchers. They have become progressively more excited as the research has unfolded, guiding them more and more towards the view that babies do not, after all, have to learn to see. Rather they have to learn to interpret what they see. It used to be thought that the atoms of vision had to be painstakingly put together from scratch - that over the first weeks and months babies had to learn, for example, that lines and angles can be viewed together as shapes or that a hand coming towards you is not really growing in size but moving in distance. Thousands of experiments have chipped away at that notion and pushed psychologists towards the view that babies start with a much more coherent view of the world.

Perhaps they do not, after all, see the place as full of shifting lines and dots where shapes miraculously grow and shrink, appear and disappear. Perhaps they see the pattern in objects and events from the start? It would, certainly, be a faster and more economical way to learn. Think of how a child learns to read. Teachers used to think the best way was for them to learn each letter of the alphabet first, then, once that was mastered, the child could go on to build the letters into words. Later educationalists realized a better way was by word recognition. Since then children have been coming home with their word tins stuffed with papers marked 'Ben' and 'Lad', 'boy' and 'dog'. They have been learning words in whole chunks, sometimes six at a time, and they can get on to their first reading book within weeks. In other words they recognize the pattern of a word before they know the individual elements which make it up. That is the position on vision that psychologists are moving towards.

This 'pattern first, detail later' approach is shown quite nicely by the early face experiments. When you look at a face your eyes focus on one point after another, darting between these fixation points as you scan the image. Babies, too, fixate and scan but the way they explore faces changes as they develop. In the earliest stages they concentrate on the top half of the head – the eyes and especially the hairline where the contrast between light and dark is strongest. In fact, given the choice between looking at their fair-haired mum or a dark-haired stranger, babies, almost against their will it seems, are drawn to the dark stranger with the high contrast hairline. Later, as they get better at seeing things and processing what they see, they

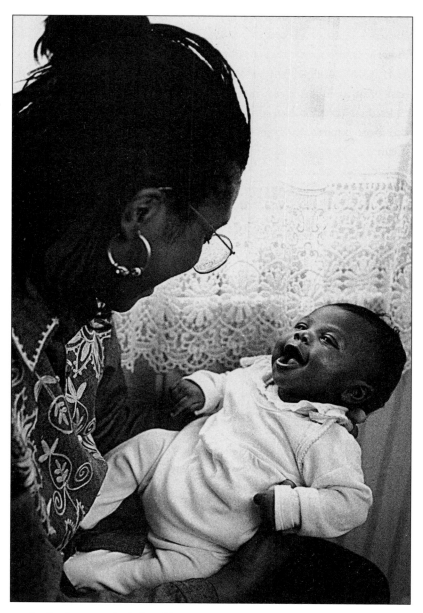

In the first months babies like nothing better than a bit of live company.

begin to look more at the inner details of the face and especially at the eyes. Later still, they will explore the mouth, nose, chin and lower features more closely.

It is the kind of pattern you might expect if you were learning first of all to tell a face from a non-face by outline and then to tell individual faces by the detail within them. That detail may not be the most important thing to the very young baby but that does not mean to say she is oblivious to it. This can be vividly shown in simple studies presenting babies with a normal face and one where the features have been totally blanked out. Babies notice that kind of thing. They miss the eyes where the eyes should be, the nose where the nose should be and so on, and they prefer to look at faces with all the usual trappings. Okay, reasoned the researchers, what if we leave the features there but just move them around? So they tried it, scrambling the features so that nose, mouth, eyes, hairline were all present but in a complete muddle. Babies did not care much for these mugshots. They preferred to look at faces where the features were properly arranged.

Going on from here to test just how sensitive newborn babies are to the finer details of the face, some experimenters have shown pictures of Margaret Thatcher to babies of only one and two days old. In some of the pictures the eyes and mouth were turned upside down – a process known by experimenters as 'Thatcherization'. To an adult this makes a face look strange but not dramatically odd. They would be hard-pressed to say immediately what was wrong. And if the faces are turned upside down they will no longer notice the 'Thatcherization' effect. Surprisingly though, babies were more sensitive to the detail than the adults were. Not only did they spot the 'Thatcherized' features when faces were the right way up, they continued to notice that something was different about them when the whole faces were turned upside down.

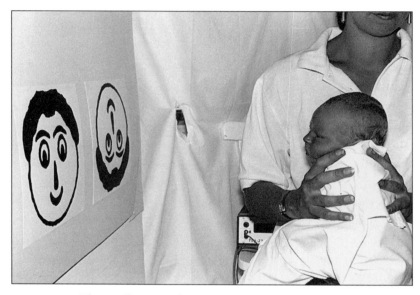

They prefer to see the eyes where the eyes should be.

What emerges from all this is that firstly babies like looking at faces rather than non-faces, then they prefer faces with features rather than those without, next they like the features to be properly arranged. More than that, researchers have gone on to find that babies would rather look at pictures of pretty women! This latest glimpse into the adult-like way in which babies see and think about faces has come from the Langlois team at the University of Texas. It came up with the unexpected – and controversial – news that, given the choice, babies as young as a few weeks prefer looking at attractive rather than plain women. What the team did was to ask students to sort a sheaf of photographs of young women's faces into those they thought were attractive and those they thought unattractive. The pictures were then shown in pairs to the babies. They preferred to look at the good-looking faces.

What does it mean? Could plain mothers be at risk of being cold-shouldered by roving-eyed children? Not a bit of it, thinks Professor Colwyn Trevarthen at Edinburgh University. He interprets babies' preferences for pretty faces in terms of the 'emotional pull of harmonious features'. When the 'ugly mums' question was aired in the Press he was quick to emphasize his belief that what this is really all about is the opportunity for sharing emotion. In a brisk letter to the *Independent* he stressed that what this shows is 'another sign that babies are born ready to have emotional responses to persons and the feelings they express... Humans learn by sharing emotions... Babies are interested in affection and "live company". In days or even hours after birth a baby learns to recognize and prefer the sight of the "mother" face, helped by immediate recognition of her gentleness, her smile and the affection in her voice.'

Meanwhile other psychologists, like Alan Slater at Exeter University, an expert on visual development, bring a different perspective to the 'pretty faces' result. They see it in terms of babies learning to categorize what they see – learning the 'treeness of tree' and what makes a face a face. They believe it might have something to do with babies forming a template of what a face should look like, and being attracted to faces which come closest to this 'average' regular face.

'The likely interpretation,' he says, 'is that babies have extracted some kind of prototype of a face from the faces that it has seen around it. If you get lots of pictures of faces and average them together, the resulting output is something that is extremely attractive. In other words the average face is more attractive than the faces that go into making it.'

However you look at it there is obviously a lot going on behind those eyes. Babies are soaking up information from what is happening around them – particularly through their eyes. It looks as if they are building up pictures or concepts in their heads, storing them, comparing new data as it comes in, and modifying the data bank as they go along. To take the analogy a bit further, it also looks as if they start not just with a set of random wires and chips but with some circuit boards already in place.

What is coming across from the latest research is that the baby arrives with a certain amount of pre-programming installed. The circuits may need a bit of environmental input to complete them but the boards are in place. There is plenty of evidence, too, that all this information-processing is positively good for the brain. Babies need input to make their brains grow just as they need food to make their bodies grow.

This rather cold computer model of the baby is, however, only half the story. Babies have an emotional side. It may not be well expressed until three or four months, but increasingly a band of psychologists are gathering support for their view that babies have some kind of emotional life from the earliest days, and that it could play an important part in driving their development. After all if babies are not passive buckets waiting to be filled, but busy little processors building up their knowledge of the world, where is the motivation for all this activity to come from? What if babies found learning fun?

It is probably less of a surprise to parents than it is to scientists that there is evidence of just that. Just as interesting as the results of the research are the experiments themselves. Time and again they have hinted that babies are not only able to solve problems, like sucking faster to change a picture, or turning to switch on a light, they actually relish these challenges. An early glimmer of this came from experiments by J.S. Watson. While studying babies' ability to learn he noticed a curious thing. When his babies cracked a problem they smiled, vigorously. It looked as if they were really pleased with themselves. The kind of problems he was looking at were fairly simple situations in which doing one thing led to another happening. For instance:

> A mobile hanging above Allia's cot is attached by a string to the baby's legs. She thrashes her body about and notices that the mobile moves. She waves her arms, and the mobile stays put. She kicks her legs and the mobile moves again. She kicks once more, watching more closely. Again the mobile moves and she beams a big happy smile.
>
> It is hard to get away from the notion that Allia is delighted to find she can solve a problem.

Mobiles are not only for fun, they help babies learn to see.

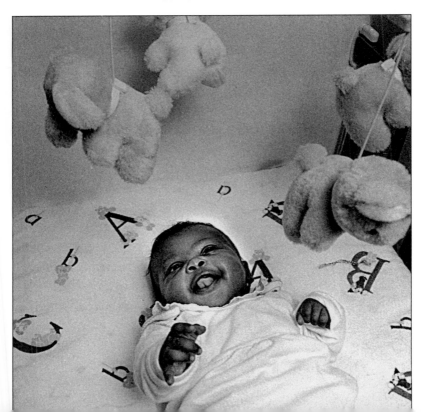

There is plenty of evidence to suggest that this is no freak experience and that babies will solve problems for no more tangible reward than the sheer joy of it. In the previous chapter we saw how newborns can quickly learn to turn their heads to switch on a light. Typically they show a burst of activity until they master the trick, then they lose interest and stop. If the problem is changed, however, so that, for example, instead of a left-head turn it is a right-head turn which switches on the light, the baby picks up interest again, turning her head busily until the problem is solved, then ceasing. Clearly the light itself is not the attraction. The fun seems to be in the baby discovering she can control something.

Czechoslovakian psychologists H. and M. Papousek have found that babies can master quite complicated problems in this way. Infants of only a few months old will learn to make a sequence of two turns to the left followed by two to the right or even a series of right-left, right-left combinations for no more reward than seeing a light turn on. When they find the solution, the babies smile and gurgle in apparent delight. At that point they also stop trying to switch the light on.

Smiling does not come under the baby's control until around the third month so it is hard to tell whether weeks-old babies might get the same kick out of problem-solving. There is, however, plenty of evidence that they do get stuck into these kind of puzzles and, given the right opportunities, they can learn very quickly how to solve them.

The evidence then is that babies can find problem-solving fun and that this might help drive the learning machine. What about babies who drop out of these experiments — those who will not co-operate in, for example, sucking to change the video channel?

In 1992 while looking into the thinking processes of young babies at Milton Keynes, John Oates of the Open University stumbled across an oddity which has opened up an extraordinary and exciting new angle on early learning. What he found takes us right back to the core of baby development – that communication-link between baby and mother. He was intrigued by the way that a few babies behave when they are in the kind of experimental situations where they are connected to a very active computer system.

'Some get very involved in it,' John Oates said, 'run it and drive it – in other words they operant-condition easily. Others get upset, turn off, throw up... whatever.'

Having worked in this field for many years, he was used to the idea that many babies never complete the course of an experiment:

'It is common experience for researchers working with young babies to "lose" up to fifty per cent of their subjects because of fretting, falling asleep, burps, possets and all the other vicissitudes of infant life,' he confirmed.

He had a hunch, however, that there was more to it than that. Working with Linda Corlett he decided to look more closely at the babies' relationships with their mothers to see if there might be a correlation with the drop-out rate. They used a sucking experiment to look at how babies learn about objects, but, in addition, they also carried out a number of tests designed to investigate how the mothers felt about themselves, motherhood and their relationships with their babies over a period of several months. The following examples are taken from a paper by Oates and Corlett, which was delivered at the International Psychoanalytic Association Conference in London March 1993.

Natalie (mother) holds Nigel (eight weeks) away from her body, on her thigh. Nigel takes the dummy and at first sleepily watches the screen. Natalie asks us 'Do you get a lot of response?' She is very muted in her behaviour, seems uninvolved with Nigel and doesn't talk to him, except after two minutes, when he turns away from the screen, opens his mouth and lets the dummy fall out. Natalie puts it back in, but he cries and does not re-engage.

'That's it, you've had enough, haven't you,' Natalie says.

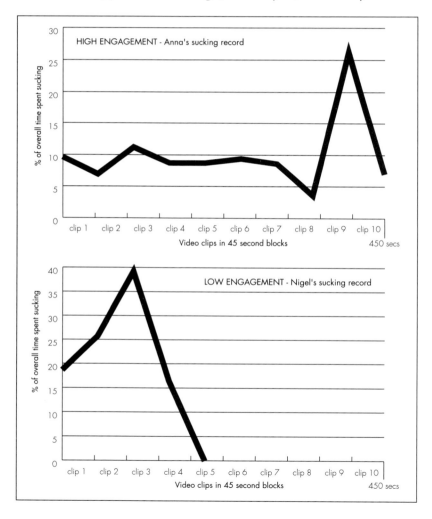

HIGH ENGAGEMENT - Anna's sucking record

% of overall time spent sucking

clip 1   clip 2   clip 3   clip 4   clip 5   clip 6   clip 7   clip 8   clip 9   clip 10

Video clips in 45 second blocks

450 secs

LOW ENGAGEMENT - Nigel's sucking record

% of overall time spent sucking

clip 1   clip 2   clip 3   clip 4   clip 5   clip 6   clip 7   clip 8   clip 9   clip 10

Video clips in 45 second blocks

450 secs

In the interviews Natalie reveals she feels 'invaded' by motherhood generally and this has brought out feelings of hostility within her. She expresses dismay at no longer being 'an individual' in 'her own right'.

In contrast twelve-week-old Anna was an example of a highly engaged subject:

> Anna starts by happily sucking on the dummy and watching
> the pictures appear – her mother Erica, also stares intently at
> the screen. After some minutes Anna starts to spit out the
> dummy. Erica says to Anna 'What's the matter?', supports her
> with her arm, and comments: 'I don't think she likes the
> dummy.' However, she continues to hold the dummy in
> Anna's mouth and they both continue to watch the screen.

'I love every minute of being a mother,' Erica says and she describes their relationship as one of warm mutual reciprocity where Anna is progressively communicating more effectively.

What the researchers found was startling. Broadly, mothers who are happy to be mums have babies who take to the task and 'engage' well with the computer. The babies who drop out tend to have mothers who are unhappy or dissatisfied with being a mum. This is not to say that 'it is all mum's fault'. It could be that babies who do not engage well tend to bring out the negative side of mothers – a point which we will look at again in chapter five. Is there a message here for real life? Psychologists are cagey to commit themselves but at a 'rule-of-thumb' level, the implication is that happy mums make for happy babies.

John Oates: 'There are definitely signs of association between mother's state of mind and whether or not a baby will engage with this rather novel experience when they suddenly find themselves driving a computer system. I think that the extent to which mothers give babies a sense of agency in the relationship has something to do with the baby exploring their own agency – or feeling confident to explore their own agency – in other areas of their experience.'

'A sense of agency' – what does that mean? Wrapped up in the phrase are notions of selfhood, of empowerment, of confidence, of helping the baby realize that she can do things which have some effect on what is going on around her, and that 'sense of agency' comes via the mother. In other words we are back to that link between mother and baby. It is beginning to look as if that bond might shape, not just how the baby responds to mum, but a good deal more. Taking this idea to the bold and simple level which brings out the nervous twitch in the academic, a good and happy dialogue with mum helps from the very start to build a baby ready to take on the world.

It also looks from this research as if babies are picking up emotional cues as well as lines, angles, movement and patterns in their environment.

To explore these two avenues a bit further – the sensitivity to emotion and the link between the baby's performance and the mother's state of mind – Oates's team did a further study in 1993. This time the team extended its view to see how postnatal depression might come into the picture, something we will look at more closely in chapter ten. Typically depressed mothers do not engage with their babies in the way that happy mums might. Do the babies of depressed mums engage well with the computer or not? That was one side of the study.

In addition, the task itself was also geared to studying how babies pick up emotional clues. The children, who were two- to three-months-old or even younger, were shown video clips of women who looked happy or sad. The videos were run with emotional voices to match but, in some cases, the emotion in the face and the emotion in the voice were mismatched so babies might see a happy face with a sad voice or vice versa. Would they notice? How would they react? The results are still being analysed as this book is being written. But, as so often happens in research, the study itself gave a fascinating glimpse of something else – that babies seem to react very differently the more the experimental situation is made to resemble 'real life'. In this case the experiment used video clips of live women and sound tracks rather than simple pictures.

'The more you make the experiment like real life the more complicated it all becomes and also the more you get from the babies,' Oates said. 'The early studies of infant perception mostly used static stimuli on the assumption that it might be possible to isolate the basic elements in visual perception. However these sorts of stimulation are very unlike the usual world of the infant, and more recent research strongly suggests babies are prepared at birth for dealing with dynamic, changing perceptual experiences.'

So, in the real world, the baby arrives with five sensory channels open, as well as what looks like the ability to read some emotional cues. Information on most events, people and objects will come through more than one channel simultaneously and yet it seems, from the laboratory studies, that babies cope – that they can read the patterns of life. Not only that, they seem to be geared to it and to thrive on the richness of life's tapestry virtually from birth.

As we are about to see in chapter three, after six weeks of soaking up information about the world – its sounds, its sights, its smells and tastes, the way that it feels – after six weeks of processing all this and building it into the system, it seems that babies may go through the equivalent of a gear change as their brains reorganize.

Fascinating Findings

One of the very first sounds that every baby hears from the moment its hearing system starts working in the womb, is the mother's heartbeat. It is a constant and regular feature of the foetus's world right up until birth when suddenly and dramatically so much changes. There are studies to show that after birth, babies will change their rate of sucking to turn on that familiar heartbeat sound. Audio cassettes of rhythmical sounds such as heartbeats have been on the market for some time for parents who want to try their pacifying effects on babies.

The suspicion that skin contact might be important to tiny babies led hospitals to swap cotton sheets for lambswool 'snugglers' in the cribs of premature babies. Being soft, lambswool lets babies sink into it, giving more skin contact than on an ordinary sheet. Babies seemed to thrive on the change – they cried and moved less and put on more weight. Lambswool fleeces are now a regular feature in premature baby units.

New babies can tell the difference between strong smells such as vinegar, liquorice and alcohol. They will even screw up their faces and turn away from nasty smells.

Newborn babies can see in colour, but because their colour vision is immature the hues tend to have a washed out look. Their favourite shades appear to be reds. Newborns also prefer to look at images where the contrast is high, for example black lines on a white background.

⬛ Babies pay attention to something longer if they are held upright or half reclining. Researchers twigged this after finding that their subjects regularly fell asleep during experiments when they were shown pictures while lying on their backs.

⬛ Young babies seem to prefer looking at things which are neither too simple nor too complicated. Given the choice between geometric shapes with five, ten or twenty corners, newborns are likely to choose the ten-cornered. How complex they like their pictures also seems to change with age. One study showed that babies of one month preferred 2 x 2 check patterns while two-month-olds preferred 8 x 8, and three-month-olds liked 24 x 24. It could be that as their vision improves they are ready to handle more difficult pictures.

What you can do with your baby

You're Never Too Young For Your First Book

Putting some of the research on babies' vision into practice, children's publishing specialists Ladybird recently launched a series of cot books specially designed for babies from birth up to six months. Using findings from The Cognitive Development Unit in London, The University of Aberdeen and the University of California, Ladybird put together a range of books taking into account the baby's visual development from the first weeks. Its *First Focus* series starts off with padded cloth books designed to be strung across the cot so junior has scope for some interesting eye exercise

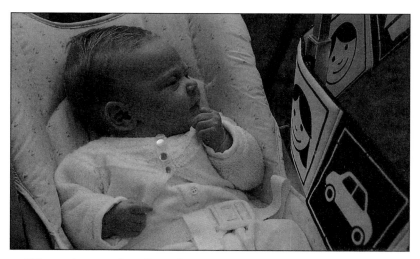

What makes a good read? Stark contrasts and simple shapes at this age.

whenever she is awake. The 'pages' show bold patterns and shapes in the thick black and white lines which attract young babies' eyes and help them to develop their visual powers. Curved lines, bold checks, spirals and simple shapes like heads and diamonds are among the images used.

Baby Can You Tell The Difference?

Babies know their mother's smell from their earliest days. Breast-feeding mothers can see this for themselves in the following way:

Take two breast pads and express some milk into one of them. Now, with your baby (preferably hungry) in a baby-relax chair or lying comfortably with her head free to turn, place the pads one on each side of her head while you stay behind her and out of sight.

Which way does she turn? Now reverse the pads. Which way does she turn? Do this several times until a pattern emerges. She should turn her head more often towards the pad with her mother's milk as she smells the difference. You could try comparing her reactions to breast milk and cow's milk in this way. It is important to reverse the pads though as young babies have a natural inclination to turn their heads to the right.

Does your baby know your voice?

With your baby sitting alert and comfortable in a baby-relax chair where she can turn her head, come up behind her and, standing to one side, say something friendly. Ask a friend to do the same on the other side. Who does she turn towards? Now change sides and try again. Does she turn her head towards her mother's voice?

Can babies see faces?

The following rather crude experiment will give you some idea:

Take two white paper plates and a thick black felt-tip pen. Draw a few straight lines on one and a face on the other with hair, eyes, nose and mouth. Now, with your baby alert and in her relax chair, show her the plate with the lines at a distance of about 30 centimetres (12 inches). Watch her watching it and, when she stops taking an interest and looks away, take it away. Present it again a few times until she is looking at it less and less. Then show her the face plate. How long does she look at it? Does she look at it for longer than the lines? Does she notice the difference between the plate with the lines and the plate with the face?

CHAPTER 3

A Gear Change: the Crying Game

In their second month babies stay awake a little longer, usually in the evening, and they are beginning to stretch the time between feeds. For many babies, however, this extra waking time is a time to cry. Whether they are brought up in swamps or in suburbs babies seem to build up to a crying crescendo when they are about six weeks old. Psychologists have found that over their first few weeks the time babies spend in this fretful state increases to a peak and then gradually declines. Not all babies are the same – some cry hardly at all, while others seem to do little else – but the average baby, if he exists, clocks up a regular two or three hours crying time daily, mostly delivered in an evening performance.

The remains of the evening meal are still on the table. There's a pile of ironing to be done and a huge mound of washing is threatening to take over the kitchen. The floor needs hoovering and mum, worn out from broken nights, just wants to curl up on the sofa and sleep. But – 'Waa-waa' – it's that time again. Evening. And evening for Daniel means crying time. Daniel, like many six-week-old babies, does not seem to settle after his tea-time feed. He's a good baby through the day – sleeps well and enjoys a kick in his cot

Most babies throughout the world reach a crying peak at about six weeks old.

and a cuddle – but in the evening, his mother jokes: 'He turns into a werewolf', fretting and fussing, sometimes for three hours at a time.

'I tried feeding him and rocking him. I tried singing and all the other things you do but nothing seemed to work,' said Gale. 'He just grizzled on and on. It wasn't like he was in pain, just not very happy.' Then, quite by accident, she discovered a solution.

> I was carrying him about in his carrycot and I thought This place is such a mess I must do something... So I laid the cot on top of the washing machine while I loaded it up and set it going. It was miraculous. As soon as the machine started, he stopped crying. By the time the cycle was in full swing he was out for the count. He'll slumber his way through 'whites', 'non-fast coloureds'... the lot... though he's not so good on 'woollens', I think the cycle's too short!

Settling your baby on the washing machine is probably not to be recommended. Some machines are jumpy and could dislodge a carrycot, but Gale's experiences is not so unusual. Most babies stop crying when they are picked up but, parents have found some idiosyncratic solutions for those determined grizzlers who will not be pacified in the usual ways. Some find starting up the Hoover calms their babies. Other couples report night drives round and round the block to get cranky babies off to sleep. According to psychologists this is not all as wacky as it might seem. Continuous 'white noise', such as the hum of a washing machine, the buzz of a Hoover or car engine, does seem to pacify babies. Tapes of heart-beats, intra-uterine noises and whale calls all have the soothing effect of rhythmic, low-pitch, continuous sound. In fact, until babies are about three months old, such noises are often more calming than mother's voice. At around that age though, the nature of crying itself seems to change. Instead of being something apparently out of the baby's control – in the sense that they do not seem to be 'doing it on purpose' – a premeditated element seems to creep in. Crying becomes more a method of communication. Mothers notice that the crying stops when the baby hears them coming as if he was thinking, 'Oh good, that's done the trick'!

In the earliest stages, however, crying is not like that – in fact sometimes it is better described as fretting and fussing. The fact that it seems to run to a pattern, happening mostly in the evening, and does not seem to be associated with good or bad parenting, has exercised psychologists' imaginations. After testing and rejecting the standard explanations to do with mother's end-of-day tiredness affecting the quality of her milk – bottle-fed babies cry just as much – psychologists have been looking elsewhere for answers.

For the last six years London researcher Ian St James Roberts has been studying crying babies in Northamptonshire and London. Using electronic bugging devices he has listened in on the daily howls of hundreds of babies to find out when and how much they cry. What he has found has led him to believe that the crying peak could be the baby equivalent of 'jet lag'. Surprisingly he is coming round to the idea that the six-week grizzles could be just a fact of life.

It is his view that babies go through an enormous internal upheaval – something like a gear change – at around six weeks old. Their brains are reorganizing to cope with a night/day rhythm and, instead of waking and sleeping on a four-hour cycle, they are moving towards a more mature state which will allow them to stay awake for longer spells throughout the day and sleep more at night. The theory is that, just as adolescents go through a grumpy and sleepy stage when they have a lot of new things going on in their bodies, babies too feel fatigued and cranky with all this extra reorganization taking place inside.

Parents, it seems, can do little about this early crying peak and may just have to learn to live with it. Now, instead of concentrating exclusively on why babies cry at this stage and how to stop them, much of St James Roberts's work is on finding ways of helping parents cope with crying.

'I think we are heading towards a rethink about crying – moving away from the idea that it reflects a disturbance or an illness and towards the idea that it is something that most babies go through. They are coming out of the uterine environment, coping with major changes, major reorganization in everything that they're doing in these early months. The job of the parent is to help them through that,' he says.

He did not arrive at this position overnight. To follow the path of the latest thinking we have to do a bit of continent crossing first. The first point that researchers established is that this six-week crying peak is not a freak effect of child-rearing methods. It does not seem to matter whether babies are brought up in North American cities, in Scandinavia or among tribes of African hunter gatherers, they show the same crying pattern. There are two ways of measuring the amount a baby cries – by the number of times he cries or by the duration of the crying spells. Perhaps what changes over those first few weeks is not how many times babies cry but how long the crying goes on?

In checking this out Canadian Ronald Barr focused on a hunting gathering people in Botswana called the !Kung San (the ! represents the clicking sound in their language). Their way of life has changed little over hundreds of years and the chances are that they have been bringing up their babies in much the same way that generations of hunter gatherers have before them. Their approach to parenting is dramatically different from the average Western family. Mothers are super sensitive to their babies. Every whimper is attended to at once.

Plenty of skin-to-skin contact, fast responses by mum and virtually continuous breastfeeding are among the benefits enjoyed by slung babies.

The !Kung San women carry their infants around with them all the time, upright in slings, with plenty of skin-to-skin contact. On average Barr noted that mothers responded to their babies within ten-to-fifteen seconds of every peep, an astonishing ninety-two per cent of the time! Often what they do is to offer a nipple, so the babies feed in an almost continuous way, sucking in short bursts every fifteen minutes or so. What Barr found was that under this baby-centred system the !Kung San infants showed that same peak pattern at six weeks, and cried the same number of times as babies in Western societies but for only half as long.

'This strongly confirms the theory we're arriving at from Western society studies that babies cry because they are somehow hard-wired to cry,' he says.

Why should the !Kung San babies quieten sooner? Could carrying be the answer? Barr tested this theory in a study in Montreal. He found the effects were striking. By carrying their babies around in slings Canadian mothers cut their crying by almost half. Confident that they were on the right trail, Barr and St James Roberts embarked on a similar study in London. One group of mothers carried their babies in slings for an average of four hours a day more than usual. A second group were primed to be extra sensitive to their babies, stimulating them and responding to them more than they would normally — this included giving them an extra feed and extra holding time. A third group were the controls who simply kept a diary.

'The mothers were very kind. They did all that was asked of them but it had no effect at all — that was a big surprise. We did expect it to work but it didn't seem to matter what the mothers did, the babies cried just as much,' said Ian St James Roberts.

This finding seems to fly in the face of the current view that mothers who are sensitive to their babies and respond to them are 'doing the right thing'. Certainly at other stages and in other situations there is plenty of evidence that babies respond to a responsive mother. Why not here? If the six-week crying peak is a side-effect of a developmental gear change it could make sense. The researchers looked around for other evidence that this could be so. They took a glimpse at families with several children. If crying is more to do with parental inexperience you might expect second and third babies to cry less than first-borns. In fact they seem to cry just as much. It seems to fit.

The developmental argument may explain why crying should peak at around six weeks but it does not explain why some babies cry more than others. Could some babies simply be born grumpy? Temperament is certainly one of two major factors now being explored by researchers into crying. The other is colic, and here an interesting strand of research on how babies can be literally sweetened up, comes in.

It all began with baby rats. It had been well established that when newborn rats become separated from their mothers they squeal in distress. Psychologist Elliott Blass then found that a few drops of sucrose water magically silenced them (see warning below).

'The effect,' said Ronald Barr 'was very striking, almost like pushing a button. So, not surprisingly, he then went and did some analogous studies on human infants and found that if you gave babies sucrose water this reduced the crying. We wanted to replicate that study but we waited until the babies – newborns – were really howling before giving them two drops of sucrose water or ordinary water. Under the sucrose condition the crying dropped to essentially nothing within ten seconds and they stayed quiet for five-to-seven minutes.'

When the same thing is tried with babies of six weeks the effects are very much weaker. Crying may be quietened but only for a minute. So what is going on here?

'What the sucrose might be doing,' said Ronald Barr 'is to access the system that is responsible for switching crying episodes to stop. This system may not be as active at six weeks of age and that may account for why crying increases over the first six weeks of life.'

Could this be the secret of the !Kung San's success? Breast milk is sweet tasting. They breastfeed their babies almost continuously – could they be accessing this 'crying off switch' more often? The assumption here is that breast milk will act in an equivalent way to sucrose water. To test this, a study is now under way in Montreal comparing the effects of each.

So is it safe to recommend the sucrose trick to mothers?

'No.' says Ronald Barr. 'There are a lot of things about sucrose we don't know yet. We don't know whether there are better concentrations or not... or if too much of it might elicit a sweet tooth. We haven't got to the point of knowing if this is a reasonable therapy. What is helpful right now is to try and understand what the mechanisms are that account for this crying behaviour. We will know a lot more about that in the next two years or so, I bet you!'

These findings have made researchers think again about that mystifying condition which seems to affect a sizable number of babies — those persistent criers who are diagnosed as suffering from colic.

For decades parents and health professionals have argued about colic. Is it real? Is it a phantom condition invented by parents who feel bad about their babies' crying and need a reason for it? Is it just a blanket term used by doctors and health visitors who cannot think of anything else? Or do some babies really suffer from acute and mysterious stomach pains in their early lives?

If babies cry because of colic they might be expected to cry in a different way — a way more associated with pain. In the classic colic cry babies are said to pull up their knees, give sharp cries and turn red. To check this out a group of mothers whose babies have been assessed as high- or low-criers, are currently co-operating with Ian St James Roberts in another baby-bugging study and making diaries of their crying days. Meanwhile, in Montreal, they are asking the question: could it be that colic is a sign that some babies are less able to respond to sugar than normal? They are now trying the sucrose trick on colicky babies to test whether they do indeed have a different response to sugar from non-colicky babies.

While the six-week crying peak may be something parents have to learn to live with, psychologists agree that does not mean that babies' cries should be ignored. The single most effective remedy they have found is the one that comes naturally to most parents - picking the baby up. This seems to work most of the time with

There is nothing quite like a cuddle to soothe the crying.

most babies and the favourite position seems to be over the shoulder. Babies, however, are individuals. Jasmine prefers to be held with her back to the shoulder, looking out at the world. Grant likes to be held upside down under his mother's arm so that he is looking at the floor as she does the housework – 'quality control' she calls him.

The next thing most parents try is feeding – whether the cry is a hunger one or not. It seems the most natural thing when your baby is opening his mouth to bawl, to try popping in a nipple of one kind or another. The act of sucking on something – even a dummy – seems to be soothing and pleasurable for its own sake, as many a long-term thumb-sucker would testify.

One study took sucking to the ultimate test to find how effective sucking is in calming babies who are crying with pain. It followed babies of two weeks who had their heels pricked for blood samples and babies of two months who had just been given injections. Dummies were almost immediately effective in stopping their crying. However the crying started again as soon as the dummy was removed. Only if the baby had fallen asleep before the dummy dropped from his mouth, did he stay quiet. Instead of being given a dummy, some babies were swaddled up tightly in a blanket. This too seemed to stop the cries and had the advantage that when unwrapped, the babies did not start crying again.

Are extra feeds the answer? Apparently it is not that simple. From the work of Ian St James Roberts and Ronald Barr it seems there might be some relationship between sucrose and a 'cry-stop mechanism', but it is more complicated than simply giving a feed to stop crying. This is also the experience of childfeeding expert Gill Harris in Birmingham. She believes you cannot 'pad up' a baby to stop it from crying. In testing a special milk formula made to satisfy hungry babies she has found babies will not be easily duped.

'The formula,' she said, 'is made to curd up in the stomach. This should delay gastric emptying thus giving the baby the signal that its stomach is full so it doesn't need any more to eat. But human physiology is more subtle than that. If you stop them taking the number of calories they need to grow, they just feed much more often. This appetite-regulation mechanism is already beginning to work by about six weeks.'

There is something very soothing about sucking.

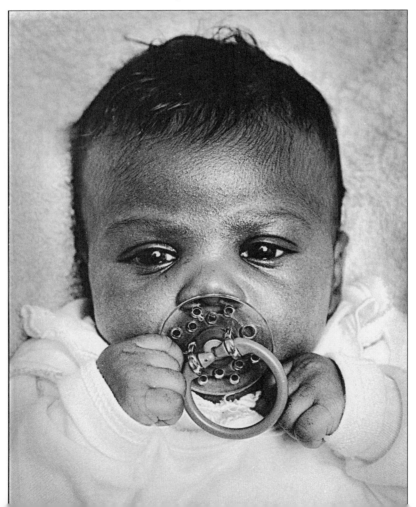

Another standard approach to calm a crying baby is to try the soothing effect of a gentle rocking motion. That, too, is something even the earliest civilizations with their swinging cribs, were aware of – and if today that rocking comes from a car journey or the spin cycle of a washing machine, it does not alter the principle.

What answers such as holding, sucking, rocking, swaddling and white noise have in common seems to be some element of low-level but continuous stimulation. Why this should act as a soother is a riddle that has yet to be solved. Some might argue that all of these have a back-to-the-womb component which might comfort babies by imitating 'the good old days' before they were pushed out into the world. It could also be argued that something continuously bombarding the senses somehow uses up the baby's limited input channels, effectively producing its own white noise in the system.

What actually works in soothing crying babies changes rapidly. Showing a crying baby a toy, for example, which in the earliest days is virtually useless as a pacifier, starts to become quite effective at around three-to-four months. This is when the nature of the cry itself seems to change from giving a message about the baby's basic states, to something with a more communicative element. How much can adults read from a cry? Do babies have different cries? 'That's a tired cry,' is a phrase mothers and grannies have been using for generations but are they right? Can they really pick up from a baby's cry how he is feeling?

It seems that babies do cry in different ways for different reasons. A hunger cry sounds different from a cry of pain or anger. A cry of frustration sounds different from a cry of distress. Most adults, and even some quite young children, can identify different kinds of cry. Even adults who have no children of their own seem to be able to spot the difference. So what are the cues?

One of the things that makes the pain cry so distinctive is the way the baby holds his breath in the middle. He starts with a high-pitched yell exhaling as he goes. Then there is a long pause – long enough to give the listener the impression that the baby has stopped breathing – before at last he inhales again. Pitch, breath-holding, intensity and rhythm of cries all seem to be important in telling us what lie behind them. In addition every baby has his own special way of crying and parents usually learn quite quickly to tell their own baby's cry from that of a stranger. They also learn to 'read' their own baby's cries and what seems to work best in soothing them. So it seems that crying could be a significant channel of communication.

The evidence also points to the fact that if babies are 'hard-wired' to cry, adults are also 'hard-wired' to respond.

Sitting on a train recently I was joined by two young men in business suits. People around us were talking, coughing and playing their personal stereos unremarked. When a baby several seats away began to cry, the men showed signs of agitation within seconds. They had not commented on any of the other distracting noises but they clearly found the sound of the crying baby difficult to ignore.

There is no doubt that adults react in a physiological way when they hear a baby cry. Numerous studies measuring heart rate, skin conductance and other signs of tension show that non-parents, as well as parents, are physically affected by babies crying. It seems that when we hear babies cry – whether they are our own or other people's – we are primed to react. Perhaps that is what makes crying so difficult to ignore.

Is this something which affects women differently to men? The traditionalists might like to think so but there is little evidence that women are biologically better primed to cope with babies crying. Men and women respond in much the same way. There are hints though that child-abusers show a different physiological response from non-abusers. They seem – according to measures of their heart rate and skin conductance – to get more worked up and they report feeling more annoyed by the noise. Curiously they respond in much the same way to a smiling baby as a crying one. It has been suggested that, perhaps because of some experience in their past, any cue which invites them to interact with a baby – whether smiling or crying – is likely to provoke negative feelings. Ultimately these bad feelings can end up in abuse.

Should babies be left to cry?

'Waa-waa-waaa.'

Maria jumps up from her meal at once and picks up little Gemma whose cries have only just begun.

'Let her be. You'll only spoil her. She's got you wrapped around her little finger,' says Granny.

This is a scenario re-enacted daily. The idea that babies are some-how 'trying it on' when they cry is commonly held, and those who believe that babies are really engaging in a power struggle with par-ents usually are the first to say 'Don't give in to them'.

Can babies be spoiled by lifting them every time they cry? That is a question many a parent would like answered. Psychologists are still arguing this one out. They cannot agree whether a prompt response reinforces crying or helps to stop it. The learning theorists would say that babies will cry more, not less, if you attend to their cries. Their logic is that babies learn that it is an effective way of getting what they want. Taken to the extreme they argue that if a baby finds that crying gets him nowhere, he will stop crying.

Reports from visitors to dismal Rumanian orphanages where babies are left in rows of cots virtually unattended for long periods of time seem to bear this out. Crying does fizzle out but such babies become withdrawn, apathetic and unresponsive – hardly a triumph for those championing this approach.

The other camp takes the view that parents who react quickly and sensitively to their babies' cries invest their children with a 'feel-good-factor'. These babies feel more secure and happy with their parents, so they cry less.

Certainly from his experience of hundreds of crying babies, Ian St James Roberts takes the view that babies should not, on the whole, be left to cry for more than about five minutes:

'Early on everything we know suggests they don't cry on purpose, they're not spoiled, they're not getting at anybody. Crying is not even under voluntary control early on. So my guess is that to begin with you should not leave babies to cry very long – and actually mothers don't by and large.'

It is hard to prove which approach is 'right' – and both sides produce evidence which they say supports their claims – but the 'early-response approach' is one which is in harmony with the current emphasis on the importance of the mother-baby link. Probably just as importantly, it is also the approach which many mothers intuitively feel is right.

Crying itself seems to change in nature as babies mature and develop. After about three months – some say even younger – babies seem to use crying, at least partly, in a way that suggests they have some notion of purpose.

At six months Paddy would yell with all his might when he was put down in his cot in the evening. His parents would time him. After two or three minutes of high-decibel bawling he would suddenly stop and go quiet. Within minutes he would be asleep.

The crying bout did not fizzle out gradually. It ended as distinctly as someone snapping off a switch. If, however, within that bout of crying, Paddy heard the tell-tale sound of the downstairs door opening, he would stop yelling for a minute, and if nobody came he would start again.

In his first weeks Paddy's mother barely let him whimper without picking him up:

'It seemed like the right thing to do. But when he got older I could tell his crying was different – it wasn't like true distress, just a "I don't want to go to bed" cry and there was a distinct pattern. I knew he would stop within a few minutes. If on the very odd occasion he didn't I would certainly go and see why.'

Like most mothers her responses gradually changed, mirroring the changes in her baby as he got older. If there is one thing that comes through in the research it is that this mother-baby dialogue is not static. It is dynamic, growing and changing as the relationship between developing baby and mother grows and changes. How mum reacts to baby affects how baby responds to mum, which in turn affects her response... And one of the elements which makes the biggest impact on this rapport is the development of the baby's smile.

Fascinating Findings

Babies each have their own unique 'cryprint' or way of crying which can be used to identify them in much the same way as a fingerprint or footprint. Parents usually learn quite quickly to recognize their own babies by their cries.

Unusual cries can be used by doctors to diagnose abnormalities, such as respiratory problems. Babies with breathing problems tend to cry at a higher pitch than normal babies. Babies cry in a different way according to whether they are hungry, angry or in pain. Most adults, whether they are parents or not, can tell the difference, but parents can read the cries of their own babies better than those of strangers.

Crying babies move about six times as much as non-crying babies. Over an hour researchers have recorded an average of 12,000 body movements in a crying baby.

Babies of under four months usually cry with their eyes closed. After four months they often cry with their eyes open.

Infants rated as 'difficult' tend to have particularly irritating cries characterized by long pauses between the cry sounds. This makes them sound as if they have stopped breathing – a pattern which lends the cries a greater sense of urgency.

A study by Moss in 1967 found that boys are harder to console when they cry than girls.

According to researchers at the University of California, women who go to exercise classes six-to-eight weeks after giving birth may increase the protein levels in their breast milk – a good thing for their babies. The scientists recently gave the thumbs-up to moderate daily aerobic exercise for breastfeeding mothers – even recommending it for women who were previously leading fairly sedentary lives.

What you can do with your baby

Getting Control

By two months babies are beginning to show a little more control of their bodies as you will appreciate with the following exercises:

- Lie him on his tummy and he will be able to lift his head to free his nose and mouth for breathing.
- When you pull him to a sitting position he will be able to hold up his head for about a minute.
- Touch his hand with a rattle, or something which interests him, and he may jerk his hand towards it – the beginnings of reaching.
- The stepping reflex will be fading away as you will see if you hold your baby upright with his feet on the table.

The signs are very subtle but if you look very carefully at your baby's fingers, toes and face you may be able to detect a difference in the way he reacts to mum and dad. Often he will respond to mum more smoothly and calmly than to dad, stretching out his fingers, toes, hands and feet towards her and pulling them back in a cycle of movement, maybe four times a minute, as his face brightens gently. With dad his responses are likely to be more jerky and excited, and his body stiffer. The tempo speeds up, his face looks more lively and his fingers, toes, arms and legs all jerk out towards dad as if expecting to play. The difference in his reactions seems to reflect the differences typically seen between the relationships with parents – Mum in a nurturing role, Dad in a playful one.

Cry-sis

Twenty thousand mothers a year — that is over fifty every day — are driven to such desperation by their babies crying that they contact Cry-sis. This support group for the parents of crying babies was set up twelve years ago by a group of Enfield mums who could not find the help they needed elsewhere. It continues to be run by parents who have all experienced the problem themselves and know just how hard it is to cope with an inconsolable crier. The group claims a remarkable success rate — some put it as high as ninety per cent.

'If you take success to mean mothers and babies feeling better, you could put our success rate even higher,' says Cry-sis information officer Elsie Matthewman. 'Often the mothers who phone us are at the end of their tether. They need to talk to someone right away, and we try to accommodate that,' she says. Nearly all the counselling is done by telephone but occasionally mothers are also invited to write: 'Sometimes they can express their feelings better in a letter.'

Key elements in the Cry-sis approach are listening to the mothers, putting the problem into perspective and building up mothers' confidence again. 'We like to start from the very beginning — was it a difficult birth? Sometimes a pattern begins to emerge.'

Cry-sis will also send out a checklist that mothers can go through — Is baby too hot, too cold? Is the room too light or too dark? Is there too much or too little stimulation?

'We never tell mums what to do but we can give advice and suggest things to try,' says Elsie.

Cry-sis can be contacted first on 071-404-5011 from where callers will be given a local number.

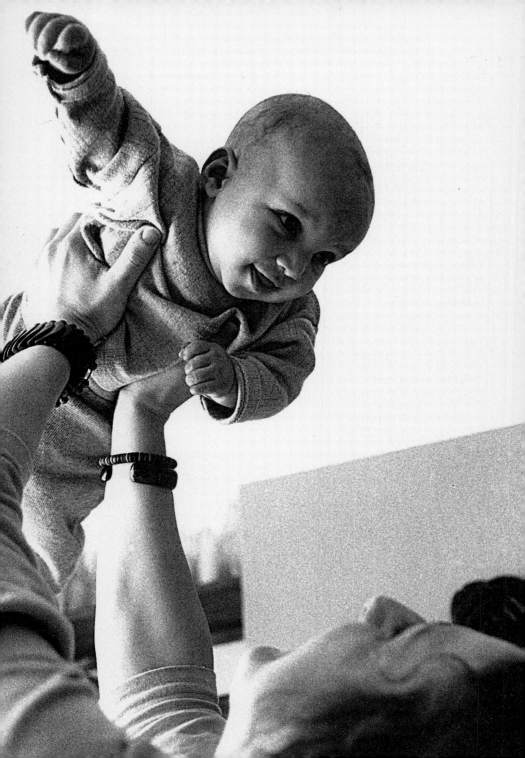

CHAPTER 4

Smile and the World Smiles with You

At three months old babies are beginning to hold their heads steady, to swipe at nearby objects and get a real taste of life by putting everything in their mouths. The most engaging development at this stage, however, is the way they 'smile-talk'.

Three month old Ajay kicks her fluffy socks in the air and smiles up at her mother. It's brief but that's a smile all right. Its effect is instant. Mum doesn't just smile, she beams right back.

'Well, hallo, Piglet. You're looking happy this morning.'

Ajay looks straight into her mother's eyes and smiles again.

'That's right,' chirps mum, her eyes exaggeratedly wide, and a huge grin on her face. 'You're having a little work-out there, aren't you?'

She pauses long enough for Ajay to smile in reply. Then she grins again.

'Step aerobics, is it?'

Ajay gurgles, kicks and smiles back, her eyes still fixed on her mother's.

They've got a real thing going between them.

A bit of body language.

Then mum plays a lousy trick. She breaks off this lovely smile-conversation and holds her face in a neutral, unexpressive pose.

Ajay smiles on for a few seconds. No response. She tries again. No response. She stops smiling and looks away. After a few seconds she steals a glance back, but mum's face is still stony and unresponsive. What has happened here? Increasingly agitated, she looks away for longer this time, squirming her body to the side. Ten seconds pass. She glances back for just the tiniest of looks. Mum's face is still a blank. Ajay screws up her face and cries.

It was with this kind of 'still-face' situation that, in the 1980s in Edinburgh, psychologists Lynne Murray and Colwyn Trevarthen demonstrated convincingly that from a very early stage babies are super sensitive to how adults react to them. By capturing inter-changes like these on videotape they could show, in a way that no amount of reported observation ever could, that babies were acutely aware of their conversation partner's response.

This 'still-face' situation is one which babies find remarkably upsetting. The adult they were getting along with just fine suddenly cuts them dead. Just as they are getting the hang of this dialogue business, the rules change and it all seems to be out of their control. Interestingly mothers, too, find the 'still-face' situation difficult and even upsetting. Most try to make it into a game – coming alive again with a 'peek-a-boo' or something to make the baby smile.

'It seemed a bit of a mean trick... a bit like putting the phone down on someone mid-conversation,' said Ajay's mother. 'I wanted to give some hint to Ajay that I wasn't cutting her dead – that it was only a game. It was a great relief to give her a big smile and a cuddle at the end.'

These smile-conversations are clearly big social occasions for both babies and mums. Both gear their behaviour towards them.

The earliest smiles, however, are not quite like that. Social smiling, like Ajay's is something which usually develops from around three months. Before that smiles seem to be more of a reflex. The youngest of babies will give a mouth-only smile, often when falling asleep – just like adults sometimes give a spasmodic jerk of the muscles when they are nodding off. Parents sometimes interpret this as 'having a nice dream'.

In the early stages, too, babies are fairly undiscriminating about who and what they smile at – a Mr Blobby face, a tinkly bell, a soft stroke, a fluffy duck. At six weeks if you show a baby a pair of black dots she will smile. If you show her two pairs of black dots she will smile more. Six black dots will have her positively beaming – more so, even than at her mother's face. Why should this be?

If smiling in the early stages is a reflex to something like a pair of eyes, then six dots – or three pairs of eye-like things – could be seen as a super stimulus drawing more smiles than any one pair of eyes, even if they belong to mum. Curiously, the strange case of the 'six-dot smile' has evaporated by the time the baby is four months. At that age, the dots will not do. It takes a face to get a smile out of a baby. So what has happened in between?

It is in this spell that smiling seems to switch from being largely a reflex to being a social act. The baby has become more choosy about what and who she will smile at. She discovers that dots are really rather unsociable things. No amount of smiling – even to three pairs – gets so much as a peep of conversation out of them, so she gives up on the dots and keeps her smiles for those who appreciate them, and particularly for those who talk back.

Premature babies are an interesting case. They lend their weight to the idea that the first smiles are pre-programmed. While babies born to full- term smile at six weeks, premature babies smile later. If, however, you measure the time at which they smile in relation to when they are conceived – the time-lag is the same, that is forty-six weeks from conception.

What about blind babies – when will they smile? Or will they? If they cannot see anyone to smile to, or to return their smiles, why should they smile at all? In fact their first smiles seem to develop around the same time as sighted babies, but their social smiles do not happen until much later. Blind babies continue with the mouth-only smiles well after the three-month stage but, interestingly, they do move on. Even though they never see anyone return their smiles, somehow, they still develop that fully-fledged smiling dialogue by about six or seven months. It looks as if denied one channel of communication they plug into another.

The earliest smiles may be reflexive but that does not mean they are of no social value. Mum certainly responds to them as if they are special and the baby notices that. From about two months plus, babies smile, wave their arms and 'talk' more to their carers than they do to toys or other babies, or even to pictures of faces. They have obviously learned something about who and what to socialise with. They have discovered Teddy's limitations in the conversation department. They have come to the conclusion that you cannot expect much sense out of just another blanket-waving baby. And pictures? Well, they can be good to look at but their line in chat is worse than talking to the bedroom clock. There is nothing quite like a good chinwag with mum – or dad. Babies take part in these chats just like an adult might – waiting for pauses before putting in their own twopence worth – giving a burst of smiles, then stopping as if to say: 'It's your turn now'.

This turn-taking is one of the fundamental things which give conversation its special see-saw rhythm. You say something. I respond. You reply to that … and so on. The idea of turn-taking, some argue, comes with the mother's milk. Some even argue that while they are suckling babies are really sending their mothers messages in a kind of Morse code. Let me explain. Most baby mammals when they suck, do so steadily and mechanically, as if filling up a tank, but not human babies. They suck in a distinct pattern – a burst of sucks followed by a pause, then another burst of sucks and another pause.

On the face of it, the idea may seem whimsical, but the suggestion has been made that this suck-suck-pause routine mirrors the rhythm of a conversation. Most mums agree that feeding – whether by breast or bottle – is a very special time when they feel particularly close to their babies. Certainly at this stage sucking from the breast is the baby's strongest link with mum. Just think of the sensory channels involved – the taste of her milk, her special mum smell, the feel of her holding you close … perhaps even the feel of her skin, the sight of her, and the sound of her voice as she says the gentle sort of feeding time things mums do. No wonder this is a special occasion. In addition the baby's part in it, sucking, is one of the few physical actions well under her own control. It certainly would be a golden opportunity for trying the first stab at a parley, but it takes two to tango. If some kind of conversation of the body is really going on, you could expect mums to make their replies in the babies' pauses. There seems to be evidence that they do just that.

His mouth firmly attached to his mother's nipple, Ben waves his left hand in the air, the fingers spread out, then lands it inaccurately on the breast above him, fingers trailing along the skin. He stops sucking, his eyes are still closed. His mother changes her position slightly, speaking to him as she does so:

'Well now, was that a little wave you gave me? Are you ready for some more?' She gives him a little jiggle as if to wake him up as she asks the question. He pauses for a bit, looking up at her face, then he starts sucking again and mum saves her conversation for the next suck-break.

Studying this jiggling routine in the late 1970s, researchers Kaye and Brazelton, were surprised to find that while mothers typically said they jiggled their babies to get them to start feeding again, what actually happened was that the jiggling lengthened the pauses between sucking bouts. Babies wait until mum has stopped jiggling before they start feeding again, even if the jiggling lasts longer than the usual pause between sucking bouts. Mum and baby are adapting their behaviour to each other to produce something like a conversation through the body.

That early meshing of behaviours is one of the signs of what Colwyn Trevarthen calls pre-speech or proto-conversation. He is one of an increasingly strong band of psychologists who believe that from a very early age – within the first couple of months – babies have an active social life. More, that they are born with a comple-ment of working emotions, primed to communicate. Even in the earliest weeks Trevarthen, and others, believe that babies take an active part in an elaborate dialogue of the body of which smiling is just a fragment.

One of the world's leading authorities in this area, Trevarthen began demonstrating this dance-like early mother-baby rapport in the 1970s.

'I made a set-up with a mirror in which we could film mother and baby and see the facial expressions of both of them clearly at the same time. We soon knew we were in possession of evidence that infants were more conscious of their surroundings, aware of different things and people, and much better at communicating than most psychologists could then believe. In the last twenty years the discovery has kept me fascinated.'

He and his team filmed scores of babies while their mothers talked to them then, very carefully, they micro-analysed what was going on frame-by-frame.

'The method,' he says, 'gives a much more comprehensive archaeology of the mind than could ever be obtained by analysis of what adults on a psychoanalyst's couch say about themselves and their recalled, edited pasts.'

The idea of conversational turn-taking comes with the mother's milk. Some even argue that babies communicate with their sucking in something like Morse code.

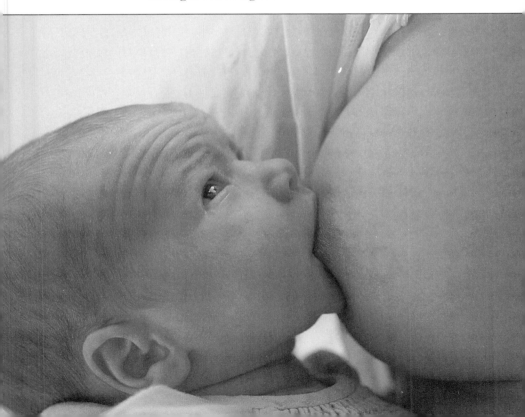

On screen the meshing of behaviours is striking. Typically the baby will work her mouth and move an arm animatedly. Then she will pause, and look attentively at mum. Mum gives her replies – verbal and non-verbal – emphasizing what she is saying with exaggerated head shakes and gestures.

The baby's whole body seems to be involved in this complex fabric of dialogue. Babies will coo, smile, turn their bodies and wave their arms animatedly in a way they do not when there is an object in front of them – it is the first attempt at a gesture. And all this is done in a pattern.

'Babies,' Trevarthen added, 'show lip and tongue movements, too, which look as if the baby is trying to articulate speech. They put a lot of effort into all this from quite a young age - six weeks or so – and they do it in an "addressing" way – they address people. They get into an address–and–reply situation which is called turn-taking.'

Contrary to what some linguists say, he believes this turn-taking is something babies do naturally.

'It is part of the way babies treat communication. It is not some-thing the baby has to learn to do. They seem to do it spontaneously just as we do.'

Some hard-boiled researchers find the idea of a weeks-old baby taking an active part in such a dialogue difficult to take on board. Okay, they say, this might look like a two-way conversation, but looks are deceptive. What is really happening is that mum is doing all the work. She is supersensitive to her baby's style, anticipating when she is about to 'speak' and getting in first. She is filling in the gaps between her baby's calls and waves to make it look like a two-way process. Arguments by mothers who say they feel as though their babies are truly responding to them are put down with the line: 'Well they would say that, wouldn't they?'

Are these 'chats' really just one-dimensional affairs – veneers carefully applied by besotted mums eager to believe that their babies are making contact? Or are they truly interactional? How could this be resolved?

Looking at natural conversations between mothers and babies was fascinating, but it was never going to prove anything. The 'Mums Rule' side had an unbeatable card up their sleeve. They could always argue that anything which looked like a response by the baby to mum, was actually an example of mum being so super sensitive to her baby that she anticipated what the baby was going to do and quickly got in an appropriate line first.

What was needed was a way of engineering the situation to throw something out of kilter and see the effects. The Edinburgh team came up with a cunning plan. It had already found the video system a fantastic tool in examining the fine machinery of communication. Now the team decided to use it like a spanner. What if they were to let mothers think they were seeing their babies live on screen, but swap some of the live tapes for replays? How would the conversations go then? If mums really are just filling in the gaps in their babies' behaviour it should not make any difference whether they see the babies live or not. In each sequence the baby will be doing exactly the same, but if these early conversations really are interactive affairs you could expect mums to behave somehow differently in the replay situation. Their babies will be producing a continuous flow of behaviour regardless of what mum is doing or saying.

What the researchers did was to set up a system so mums and babies of eight or nine weeks were in separate rooms but could see a life-size image of the other on screen. The team was careful to make sure that the partners could make that important eye-to-eye contact. The mothers were told this was a study about social development

*The split screen experiments showed these early conversations
were not one-sided affairs.*

and they were asked to chat as naturally as possible to their babies.
As far as they were concerned they were talking to them live via the
screen. For two of the four sessions, however, the experimenters
used the film they had taken earlier, taking care to get rid of any
clues that might have given the game away. Would there be any
difference in how the mums reacted?

The answer was quite clear. In the replays, the mums felt ill at
ease. They talked in a different way and overall their conversation
reflected their anxiety. They were more negative, saying things like:
'You're not interested in mummy, eh?' and 'I'm running out of
conversation. I can't do anything if you won't talk to mummy.'

Here are some of their spontaneous remarks in casual conversation
while still unaware of what had been going on:

'Well, in the one when I asked if she could hear (second replay) I felt she wasn't responding to me. There was a barrier, you know; it was as though I wasn't there and I just felt, well, either she's not hearing me or she's not seeing me – something, mm. At the end of the third (second live), I felt she could feel something from me, feel something. In the other it was as though something was between us and I wasn't getting through at all.'

This was convincing evidence for the case of the interactive mother and baby. A second body of evidence came from the same experiment done, as it were, in reverse. What would happen if the baby was shown replays rather than live clips of mum? How would infants react?

Again the effects were obvious. Lynne Murray reported: 'There was a marked change in the replay – the baby turned away from the image of the mother showing signs of distress – frowning and grimacing.'

The babies were clearly upset. They did not enjoy this situation. While in the blank-face setting they tried to get their mums to re-engage with them, in the replay situation they were more likely to turn away as if puzzled and confused. Mum's behaviour did not seem to match up with their own any more. They did not like this and could not quite figure it out.

It looks, then, as if both mothers and babies are highly sensitive to each other's efforts at communication. They want to 'engage' and when that communication link is dislocated in some way they notice and are upset.

So far we have looked at the physical side of this communication but what about the verbal side – the way mums and dads actually talk to their babies – does this have anything to add to the picture? The first thing that strikes any objective observer when they listen to someone talking to a baby is the way they speak. Even if they

Exaggerated expressions, sing-song tones, high-pitched sounds - baby talk is the Esperanto of international parenthood.

cannot see who is involved they know what is going on – these conversations have 'baby' stamped all over them. Mums and dads adopt a special language in their early chats with junior – babytalk. It is the Esperanto of parenthood, an international 'motherese' in which you exaggerate what you say and the way you say it. You speak more slowly in a sing-songy way. You repeat words and generally tune your conversation to how the baby is behaving. Take, for example, mum talking to three-month-old Bryony below:

'What's that you're doing, tadpole?'
Bryony wriggles in her chair and her face twitches.
'You're going to give me a smile?'

Bryony is looking up and waving her arms.
'Are you going to give me a smile?'
She's found her mouth now with her fist and she sucks it noisily.
'Are you going to smile then for mum?'
Her fist out of her mouth again, Bryony smiles and gurgles.
'Yeeees, that's right, that's right. A nice big smile. Lovely,
you're giving mum a smile.'

In Urdu, Japanese and Turkish it is the same story. Even in Mandarin Chinese, in which the tone affects the meaning attached to a word, they talk in 'motherese'. The words may be different but the script is much the same and the way it is performed varies remarkably little. It should probably come as no surprise, then, to find that babies – at least when they are two- and four-months old – actually prefer 'motherese' to what might be called normal adult speech. It is probably no accident, then, that baby songs are remarkably similar from one culture to another.

'The basic form,' Trevarthen says, 'is a four-line stanza with an andante beat, each line having four beats. Try:

Humpty Dumpty sat on a wall,
Humpty Dumpty had a great fall.
All the king's horses and all the kings men,
Couldn't put Humpty together again.

Mothers sing these songs with a pattern to the lift and fall of their voices that seems to appeal to babies from Basingstoke to Brazil. Computer studies imitating the features of babytalk have tried to tease out what it is that makes 'motherese' particularly attractive to babies. So far they suggest that one of the most important things seems to be that sing-songy quality.

What can all this early emphasis on communication mean? Psychologists link it with much of their later social behaviour. The theories vary in their detail, but what they hold in common is the view that a good relationship between a baby and her mother gives a positive foundation for her relationship later with the rest of the world. The father of psychoanalysis, Sigmund Freud, saw the relationship as based on the satisfaction of basic needs like hunger. If mum provides feeds to order she is assured of the star position in the baby's universe. Freud's disciple, Erik Erikson, interpreted the role of this first relationship more in terms of the baby learning to trust or distrust the mother first and generalize from this to the world. Later John Bowlby emphasized the innate elements in the attachment of babies to their mothers. However they differed in the detail, all three considered that mother–baby link crucial in a child's social development. What they did not account for was how babies are sociable and active little communicators from the earliest days.

This is what the Trevarthen school believe they have shown. They believe communication is at the core of the baby's development. They talk of a revolution over the last thirty years in the way psychologists view babies and the cornerstone of it is communication. This revelation Trevarthen regards as 'the most significant discovery in developmental psychology of the last quarter century'. It is his view that babies are born with emotions and a consuming interest in live company. Long before teddies, rattles and television capture their attention they are more interested in another person than in anything else in the world.

'I interpret that as being evidence for the control of development by communication,' he says.

Fascinating Findings

Girls spontaneously smile twice as much as boys in the first few weeks of life.

From about the age of three months babies' smiles come in clusters, four or five at a time, followed by a pause of maybe half a minute before the next cluster of smiles.

The Duchenne smile is the name given to that eye-crinkling grin which involves the whole face, not just the mouth. The name comes from the Frenchman of the same name who 'discovered' such smiles a century ago.

When babies smile their heart rate is declining rather than increasing or at a peak. This is taken to mean that smiling is a relaxing thing to do.

Some studies have shown that babies raised in institutions where they do not get much social stimulation smile later and less often than babies brought up in families.

The wide-eyed smile given by babies to familiar people like mum and dad is sparked off in the right-hand side of the brain. The smile given to strangers – which lacks that special eye twinkle – comes from the left-hand side of the brain.

Babies don't react to tickling before about three and a half months. Only after they have reached that age do they squirm and laugh and show signs of being ticklish. Some psychologists have suggested this could be because the baby's sense of itself as a separate person has not yet developed. This, they argue, is essential if you are to experience something as ticklish. As support for this line they say:'Try tickling yourself and you'll find it doesn't work'. You need to know someone else is involved before you feel it as ticklish.

Babies of only three months old can already match lip movements with sounds. A study by psychologists Kuhl and Meltzoff in 1982 played the babies a sound-track going 'ba ba ba' and allowed them to choose between two films. In one the actor is mouthing 'ba ba ba' and in the second the same actor is mouthing 'ga ga ga'. They chose the one which matched the sound they heard.

What you can do with your baby

The Three-month Feeding Window

Another interesting feature of the three-month stage in a baby's development is the discovery of the three-month feeding window.

At three months old many babies are beginning to have their first taste of solid food. 'Keep it bland and leave it late' was the traditional advice, but research by child feeding expert Gill Harris at the University of Birmingham looks like turning all that on its head. She claims that babies do not like bland foods. They prefer their food salted or sweet.

The sweet preference is there from birth, but the liking for salt is more surprising. As Gill Harris explains: 'This preference became evident even in babies who had never been fed solid food – though they had, of course, been in amniotic fluid which is mildly salty. They preferred salted to non-salted cereal.'

More, she believes there is a window between the ages of three and six months of age during which babies will take a range of different tastes even some quite extreme things – and what they eat then seems to set their food preferences for later:

'Going on with the testing we found that when babies get a bit older they prefer the salt level that relates to the salt levels they've had in foods a week before hand – in other words the taste that they have had before. It is very low levels of salt – salt in cheese, or in bread, that sort of thing. It would seem that whatever the taste they experience they then generalize from that. So if you want your child to eat a varied diet later, then what you do is you feed them lots of different things in that three-to-six-months period.'

After the six-month stage, however, that window seems to close and babies are much less receptive to new tastes.

'When you get on to a year,' Gill Harris added, 'they will eat foods just so, just as they normally have them, and then you start getting difficulties in introducing new foods. It seems like an end of generalization. They have decided what they are going to eat and that's it.'

By that stage they not only know what they like, but they like what they know.

Children who miss this early window are in danger of developing eating problems in their second year. Some have a range of only two or three foods which they will eat – 'and usually one of these is crisps'.

Gill Harris explains this three-month window in terms of babies learning what is eatable and what is not before they reach a mobile stage:

'All food preferences are culture-specific. They have to be taught. If you think about it we could eat the cushion on a chair, so some things are eatable and some things are foods. We have to work out what is a food, and that is set in these early months.'

The Six-dot Smile And Other Tricks

What makes a baby smile changes as she develops. At first anything like a pair of eyes will do, and the more eye-like things she sees the more she will be inclined to smile. But later she becomes more discriminating. This can be seen most clearly with her reaction to pairs of dots. To try the six-dot smile trick your baby should be less than four months old. Take a white paper plate and a black felt-tip pen. Draw a pair of blobs on the plate. With your baby sitting in her baby relax chair or on somebody's knee, quiet and alert, show her the plate at a distance of about 30 centimetres (10-12 inches). Hold it there for a minute or so. Does she smile? Now give her a rest for a little while. Meanwhile you can add another two pairs of blobs to the plate so there are six in all. Show it to your baby once more. She should smile even more this time. Put your plate away for a few weeks or months and try again after your baby has passed the four-month stage. Will she still smile for the dots?

A more sociable and fun variation on the 'still face' situation is a simple game of peekaboo without the hiding. Break off one of your smiley chats with her and keep a po-face for a few seconds. Watch your baby's reactions. Does she try to get a response out of you? After she has tried once or twice give a big bright 'Peekaboo!' Once she has got the idea you could try making your 'peekaboo' depend on her doing something particular like making a noise or waving her hand towards you.

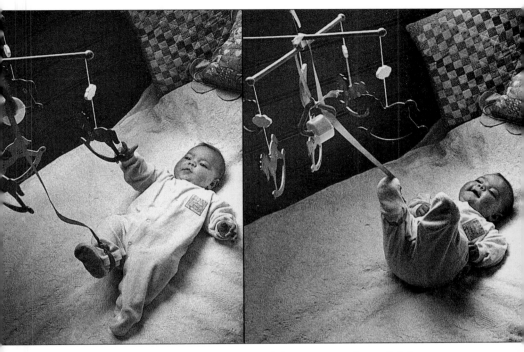

Discovering you can kick-start your own mobile is a source of great delight.

Another game which helps babies enjoy finding out that one thing can lead to another, is to shake a bell or rattle every time she turns her head to the right. Once she has mastered that, try changing the trick so she has to turn her head to the left to make the bell ring. Does she learn that more quickly? Make it fun, of course, reinforcing the bell ring with lots of smiles and nice words.

Babies of this age can also have lots of fun in discovering they can make their mobiles move. If you have a mobile above your baby's cot you could try hanging a light toy or rattle from it within swiping distance. She will have a whale of a time batting at the dangling object. If it makes a noise when she hits it, so much the better.

CHAPTER 5

The Emerging Self

At four months old babies are great companions. They squeal and laugh, cry to make someone come, explore things with their hands, maybe roll over and perhaps even sleep through the night. Parents feel they are beginning to get a glimpse of who their baby is.

Lachlan bawls, kicking his legs against the bumper panels of his cot and thrashing the air with his arms.

'You're an impatient wee blighter,' says mum. 'You like everything to be bang on time... a little boss-man.'

His eyes are screwed up, he's red in the face and his cries are coming out like bellows.

'You want your bottle and you want it now. No messing around with daft excuses, isn't that it? I can see you turning into a real Victor Meldrew,' she tells him. 'You're going to be just like your dad!'

Meanwhile four-month-old Linda is enjoying herself. Sitting on dad's lap she is entertaining a host of admiring aunties and uncles with her full social repertoire of smiles, babbles, coos and engaging body talk.

Parents are beginning to get a glimpse of who their baby is.

'You're a proper little charmer,' says dad. 'A real party animal. You just love an audience. I think you're going to be a singer.'

Linda gives one of her best gurgles and swipes dad on the chest.

'What? You're thinking of politics? No, you're too nice-natured for that... I think you're going to follow in your great grandmother's footsteps – she was an opera singer, you know – and you've got her chin.'

Big changes take place in babies between three and four months. They are awake much longer now and during these waking spells they begin to enjoy a bit of social life – engaging others in smiles, simple games and 'conversation', as well as responding to them. The four-month-old is beginning to show himself as a character, and his mum and dad react to that – they look eagerly for signs of what and who he is going to be like. They encourage, interpret, label his behaviour. Lachlan is impatient just like his dad. Linda likes an audience – a budding actress. They take what their babies do, give it shape, tell them what it means and hand it back.

What the latest research suggests is that how parents 'read' their babies – whether they interpret their smiles, their cries, their kicks, their gurgles as intentional or not - affects the way they develop. This stage where parents are actively searching for – and finding –the things that make their baby a little 'character' is just the latest stage in the dialogue that mum and dad have been rehearsing the baby through since birth.

In chapter one we saw how babies are primed from birth to 'engage' with their mums – they are drawn to her voice, her face, her smell. In chapter two we discovered that even in the first weeks babies are drinking in not just hard information about the world,

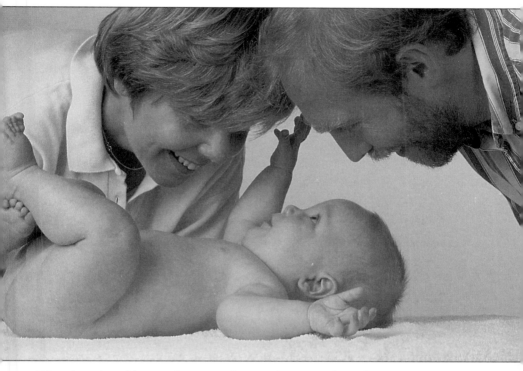

There is nothing like an admiring audience to bring out the performer in you.

they are also tuned in at an emotional level. In chapter three we saw them change gear as the brain makes a major adjustment to life outside the womb. In chapter four we saw more evidence of how sensitive babies are to emotional cues and how smiles lend a real spark to the communication link. Now the evidence is unfolding to reveal that this sensitivity goes far beyond what we might have expected. Yes, babies gear their behaviour to their mother's reactions in a simple way such as: 'That gets me a smile' or 'that seemed to turn her off' but it goes deeper than that. It seems they are also aware at some level of what their mothers think of them.

How Does It Work?

Imagine you have been given a late part in a play in which everyone else has been acting for some time. They are seasoned performers. They know their lines and their roles. You are completely raw. You don't know when you are supposed to speak, what you are supposed to say, how you should behave in the part. To bring you quickly up to performance standard one of those acting close to you is assigned as a minder. She prompts when it is your turn to speak. She says things slowly for you to repeat. She models the role you are expected to play. She draws the framework of the character you are playing with comments like: 'You're happy now... You like an audience, a proper little charmer...' or 'You're in a grumpy mood. You're telling me you want your breakfast'. And she gives you plenty of appreciation and encouragement when you get it right.

After a few rehearsals you begin to get the hang of it. You do not need her heavy-handed cues and prompts any more. You know when you are expected to speak. You have an idea of the lines that are appropriate and you begin to bring something of yourself to the role that she has outlined for you. That is roughly the stage the four-month-old is at.

Now imagine how differently you might have played the role if the minder, or mother-figure had taken another approach. Imagine, for example, that she was distant and unresponsive. You might have been slower and more hesitant in picking up your role. If instead of saying: 'You're miserable because you're hungry' she made you feel bad by saying: 'You're just crying to wind me up', you might have played out some of that bad feeling in your role.

A broad – and startling – hint as to how involved mothers may be in moulding the way their children develop came from a series of studies by a team of psychologists led by Brian Vaughn, in

Chicago, in the 1980s. The team asked mothers before their babies had been born, what they thought their children were going to be like. Astonishingly, most of the time they got it right. They could predict with a fair degree of accuracy whether their babies were going to be 'easy' or 'difficult'. Like so much in research the trail of the Vaughn team's investigation started elsewhere. It began by looking at how the mental health of a mum might affect her unborn child. Over 200 mothers were given psychiatric tests before the births of their babies, then when the children were four months old the mothers were asked to rate their temperaments. What came out of this was that anxious mums had 'difficult' babies – babies who were irregular in their eating and sleeping habits, cried a lot and reacted intensely.

The emerging self —it's just the latest stage in the dialogue that parents have been rehearsing their baby through since birth.

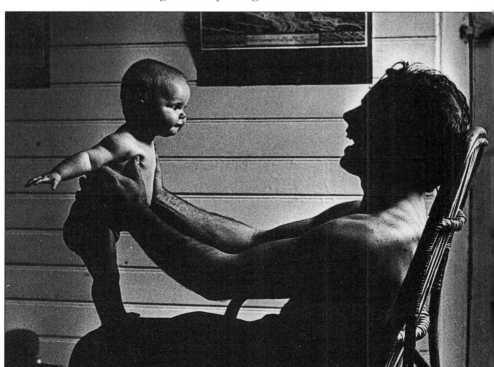

'Well, well,' said the researchers, 'what's going on here?' So they tried another study. This time they asked mums before their babies were born what they expected them to be like. Strangely enough, when the babies were rated at six months old, they matched up to their mothers' expectations before they were even born. Those who anticipated having difficult babies got them, and those who expected easy ones got them.

'Hmm,' said the critics. 'Your samples were very young – about twenty years old – and they were poor and they were uneducated. Maybe that all has something to do with it. What about a different class of mother? How would she fare?'

At this point the trail shifted to Canada where more data was collected, this time from educated mums. Would they be able to predict what their babies would be like? They would and they did. Again anxious mums expected and produced 'difficult' babies. Relaxed mums expected and produced 'easy' babies.

'Aha,' said the other camp, pulling out that well-used ace that women have come to expect in so many arguments. 'It could be their hormones.' What if the anxious mums are producing extra nasty biochemicals which are affecting their babies' temperaments while still in the womb? Could the babies be influenced by that?

Now, it just so happened that, back in Chicago, a study was under way looking at hormones, pain and pregnancy. Mums were being given a battery of physiological and psychological tests and, at various stages, they were being tapped for body chemicals. After the birth they were being followed right through the first year. Hormones they had in abundance... but no convincing link was ever found between them and the baby's subsequent temperament.

So it is back to first base – mums, it seems, can predict what their unborn baby is going to be like. Is this crystal womb-gazing or could they have a hand in shaping their infants?

Most mothers will tell you their babies were not born like super-market sausages, all exactly the same. Even in the earliest days they can see hints of each son and daughter's individuality. Some babies are more alert than others, some more active, some are more easily upset, some easier to cuddle, easier to calm... It all adds up to what the average night-rising, buggy-pushing mum would call their temperament. And most would, when still pregnant, have formed at least the glimmer of an idea about, for instance, how active their baby is and how slowly or how strongly he reacts to say, loud noises or mum having a hot bath or running upstairs. Ellen's experience is not at all unusual:

'My first baby, Douglas, was an easy pregnancy. He didn't seem to move around very much and he was quite a regular little sort – had his times for a little light exercise – mostly in the evenings. His dad said he would be a footballer, but I told him I thought he was reading a book in there, he was so quiet. That's pretty well how he's turned out. Now he's four. He's not an athlete. He likes to sit and concentrate on drawing or something... a bright, undemanding boy. But his brother is something else. Euan is an absolute toerag. He's always on the go... never still for a minute, and very demanding. And that's what he was like inside – always wriggling about. I used to balance a glass of water on my bump to see if he could knock it off!'

The different temperaments of babies is a fascinating topic and one which mums and dads never tire of discussing. They enjoy comparing their children and marvelling at the differences even within their own family. Why should babies be so different? Are they born that way or is it the way they are brought up? It is the old nature/nurture debate. As an area for scientific study it is fraught with difficulty. Problems haunt it like spectres at the feast. The first bogeyman is the definition. What is temperament? Ask a fistful of psychologists and you will get a fistful of answers. They talk about traits. They talk about 'heritability'. They talk about tendencies rather than acts. They talk about continuity over time. They talk a lot. What goes to make up a temperament? How do you measure these elements? Can they be changed? How much is genetic? Questions like these have kept psychologists round the table for years.

Numerous models and theories have been constructed, tested, dismantled and argued over... and still the waters are as muddy as ever they were. Broadly, though, the kind of features temperament researchers look at in babies are:

- Activity level: Is this a child who lies quietly for long periods or moves about a great deal?
- Emotionality: Is he easily upset? Easily calmed?
- Sociability: Does he like to engage in conversations or turn away from contact? Is he afraid of strangers?
- Attention: Is he alert and focused or easily distracted?
- Frustration: How does he react when something is beyond his limitations?

These are the focus of study but how do they go about examining them? These are not qualities to be measured in centimetres or amplitude. They must be rated, over time, by someone close to the child. Usually that means mum... and this is the second bogeyman. She is closest to her baby. She should know him best, is the logic. On the other hand, except in rare instances, she is unlikely to be the most objective observer in the world. The shortcomings of having mothers rate their own babies have been demonstrated time and again. The problem continues to leave researchers stumped. How else can they get at these baby qualities except by going via the person who knows him best?

The third spectre haunting the field is the self-fulfilling prophecy. If mothers are encouraged to think about their babies' temperaments and label them at an early age, the fear is that these labels stick. Once a baby is seen as 'difficult' he will continue to be seen as 'difficult'. It is a nightmare trying to tease out cause from effect. Even then the research might currently be pursued with more zeal if a fourth shadow had not chilled the enthusiasm. Bluntly, this was lack of strong coherent results. If early temperament tests had given a 'photofit' picture of the future adult inside, the embers of research might have been fanned to a blaze but no such results have been established. Rather the findings have been confusing, unstable and difficult to interpret. The message to parents seems to be that some aspects of a baby's temperament may be reflected in his personality later, but they can be reflected in different ways and temperament itself is not written in stone – it can be changed. The field of temperament research is muddy indeed.

Current thinking, though, has shifted from the idea that temperament is something coming entirely from the baby. Those hints we saw earlier that mothers could be playing some part in shaping their babies, strike a chord with today's chorus about the importance of the mother-baby dialogue. Today's psychologists are much more inclined to look at things in their social context. It may make the picture more complicated but it might also give a truer reflection of what is going on. They are prepared to take into account that babies do not operate within a vacuum. Infants are very much part of a twosome (at least) with the second half usually being mum. That is not to say that babies do not have their own characteristics, but they are characteristics within a context. Splitting them off to examine in isolation is like taking one of Monet's brilliantly coloured haystacks out of the sunshine and saying what do these reflections tell us about the inside workings of the haystack?

Take, for example, John Oates's findings discussed in chapter two. Put simply he found that babies with happy mothers made willing subjects in the computer game. Babies with unhappy mothers did not want to play. So, babies are affected by mums. Are mums affected by babies? Of course they are, says common sense. If a baby is bubbly and smiley and sociable you cannot help reacting to it in a different way than you would to a baby who throws up every time he looks at you, cries a lot and is impossible to cuddle.

Common sense tells us these things but scientifically they are not always easy to demonstrate. However, in Cambridge recently, a study by Professor Lynne Murray added a bit more academic weight to the argument. She found that irritable babies could affect their mothers drastically. Indeed they could play a role in triggering post-natal depression even in mothers who were not classed as 'at risk'.

For a long time depressed mothers have talked about their babies being 'difficult' in one way and another. Academics have never been sure whether to believe them. The evidence was that babies reacted to miserable mums – the 'still face' experiments described in chapter four showed us that. But could it be that they were right? That mothers owed at least some of their 'switched off' behaviour to their babies' temperaments? Professor Murray believes so. She found that after stripping out other risk factors, the mothers of irritable babies were more likely to become depressed in the first six weeks. Evidence, she says of 'The powerful influence infants may exert on those involved in their care'.

So, a cycle seems to be at work here. Babies affect mothers and mothers affect babies. We can see at a basic level how babies affect mums – a cheerful, bubbly and cuddly infant gets a different kind of reaction than a baby who turns away from contact, cries a lot and will not be comforted. We can see how that reaction can, in itself, affect the baby. But according to one group of psychologists –

known by some as the 'as if' camp – there are also influences going on at another level. They believe that the way mum interprets the baby's actions – the 'as if' element – is also an important piece of the equation. What they are particularly interested in is whether mum believes her baby is acting intentionally or not. Broadly, if mums think of their babies' eye glances, smiles and gurgles as efforts to communicate – as intentional acts – their dialogue and the babies' general development is likely to be enhanced. If, on the other hand, mums look on their babies as bundles of squirming flesh with no sense of intention about what they are doing, the dialogue and the development suffers.

Looking more closely at how mothers 'read' their babies – in effect how they see the 'self' operating within – American psychologist Suzanne Zeedyk is currently developing an exciting line of research at the University of Dundee. She was frustrated by the attitude among some psychologists that mothers are not so much 'reading' their babies behaviour as projecting their own ideas on to it. For instance, when mum says to her gurgling baby: 'You're trying to talk to me, aren't you?' – they would argue that the idea is coming from mum, not from the baby.

Zeedyk suspected that mothers were not quite the amateurs with the rose-tinted glasses that some of the academic literature made them out to be. She videotaped mothers at play with their four-month-old babies then asked them to watch the tape and stop it each time they saw their baby do something which they reckoned was intentional. What she found was that mothers used the same kind of cues that cognitive psychologists do to read their babies, but in addition they pick up on some social cues that cognitive psychologists have generally ignored. So whatever they are doing when they say 'Wee Jimmy is trying to tell me a story,' it is not pure projection.

Mothers may be reading real enough cues, but how subjectively are they reading them? As we have already seen one of the major problems in this area of research is that babies are usually rated by their own mothers, so it is hard to tell if the results are due to the baby or the mother's impression of her baby. To side-step this grave-yard of many a research study, Zeedyk came up with a rather nifty design. She put together a series of very short clips of babies – all four-months-old – doing things such as reaching for a toy, smiling at mum, sneezing and so on. She then showed the resulting film to other mothers and asked them to say, for each clip, whether they thought the baby in the film meant to do whatever he or she was doing.

'With this design,' she explains, 'you are holding the actions of the infant constant so, if there is variability, it can only be due to the parents.'

Several exciting results emerged. First, she found that depressed mothers read the babies more 'negatively' than mothers who were not depressed. In other words they were less inclined to see the baby's actions as intentional. Secondly she found that, as long as the baby was doing something non-directed like sneezing, or directed towards an object like looking at a toy, then mothers agreed about what was going on. When it came to behaviour, however, that might have been regarded as social – for example smiling at mum – a curious difference emerged between the attitudes of the mothers according to the age of their own babies. Mothers whose babies were the same age as those in the clips, that is four months, were much more inclined to think the babies meant what they were doing than were mothers of eight-month-olds.

So mothers change the way they read their babies as they get older. Does this mean that in the early stages they are so keen to see the little 'self' within their baby that they over-interpret the signs?

Or are mums really super sensitive to what is going on in the early months of their babies' development?

'It's hard to say what is happening,' says Zeedyk, 'other than it looks like a pattern. Now, of course, what I want to do is some more studies with mothers of younger and older babies.'

It is what psychologists would call an interactional model. It is not simple. At every stage a host of other influences have some bearing on what happens. For example, how the baby acts to start with will have something to do with the particular setting he is in and with the genetic inheritance he brings with him. How mum picks up on what he does, indeed if she picks up on what he does, will depend to some extent on her state of mind. How she interprets it, according to Suzanne Zeedyk's work, could also depend on the baby's age.

That interpretation itself seems to affect the baby's development. John Oates talks about the mother creating a 'psychological space' into which her baby is born and grows. Mum talks to her baby as if she understands what he is saying and she elaborates around that. In this way she builds up her own mental model of what the baby is like. She is reacting then not just to what he is doing, but also to her model of what he is like. In the example at the start of this chapter Lachlan's mum is already pencilling him roles as a 'boss-man' and one of life's Victor Meldrews. Linda's dad sees her as 'loving an audience, a little charmer'.

They are introducing potentials which the child might later explore. They are offering him a repertoire of responses which he can choose from. An equivalent kind of situation has been talked about by psy chotherapists. Their approach goes approximately along the lines of: Treat a client as though he was roughly the person he is about to become. He will explore being treated that way and will gradually fill in the personal details.

So far we have looked at the baby's emerging character from the outside looking in. What is it like from the inside looking out? Do babies feel like people? Do they have any sense of self? A tricky question this for those who like their evidence hard and usually in numbers... but a carnival for the theorists.

Jamie (four months) is lying in his cot. He is highly entertained with his latest add-on, a shiny mirror. He smiles at it. He gurgles and he tells it a long story in his own words... sometimes as long as two syllables. But what does he see there? Does he recognize that little orator with the nice line in dimples as himself?

The answer at this stage is probably not. Of course, just because he does not know what he looks like does not mean he has no sense of self. Indeed, looking at it the other way around, you are unlikely to have no sense of self if you know what you look like. In a delightfully inventive series of experiments, psychologist Michael Lewis has found a way of exploring babies' awareness of how they look. In one of his most entertaining demonstrations he had babies of nine months and over look in a mirror. Mum would pick up the baby, wipe his nose, and in the process dab it with red dye. She would put him back in front of the mirror and watch his reaction to this red-nosed reflection. Very few babies of under a year reacted to the dye. Older children touched their noses. Some even commented on it, and fifteen months seemed to be a critical age. By this time, it seems fair to say, like a butterfly from a chrysalis, a sense of self has emerged, visible in the outside world... which is not to say it has not been in the process of emerging all along.

Mirror images give a hint of the baby's idea of himself as a separate person, but they do not tell much about what he feels like

Whoozat? Making acquaintance with that snub-nosed kid with the fuzz on top can be a source of great fun to the four-month-old.

inside. Just because he cannot recognize the dribbler in the mirror does not mean he has no sense of who he is. Traditionally, psychologists have peddled the view that babies have to learn to see themselves as separate beings – they have to learn to differentiate themselves, particularly from mum. This is a notion which tends to bring out the knee-jerk 'I don't believe it' reflex in time-served mothers. It certainly does not sit comfortably with the feeling they have of a two-way dialogue batting back and forth between them.

How can babies take an active part in communicating if they feel as if they are a part of their mums? American psychoanalyst and developmentalist Daniel Stern sympathizes with the intuitive mum.

He takes the view that babies have some sense of self virtually from the start. In his opinion in their first few weeks babies have many separate experiences – they see things, they hear things, they suck things. These snapshots of life may be quite clear and vivid, but they are not seen as connected at first. Their lack of relatedness, however, is not noticed. Gradually the baby is putting the snaps together, organizing his experiences and beginning to make patterns of them. Through this very process he is building up his own sense of self.

This is what parents are beginning to see when their four-month-old smiles his special smile and starts to tell them his own story in words of two syllables.

Fascinating Findings

Babies cannot breathe well through their mouths before they are four months old because of the way their mouths and throats are adapted for efficient sucking. As they mature, however, their vocal tracts show major anatomical changes and mouth breathing is easier.

Babies whose mothers engaged their interest in objects and events at four months had larger vocabularies at twelve months according to a study by Bornstein and Ruddy.

Infants brought up in cold climates are likely to be separated from mothers at an earlier age. They do not enjoy the same amount of skin-to-skin contact as babies in hot climates and are generally kept at a distance from their parents by the use of cots, prams, buggies, baby seats and playpens. In hot climates babies are carried around with their mothers day and night and breastfed until they are older.

A surprising twenty per cent of babies are timid according to psychologists who have tested reactions to strange mobiles and unfamiliar voices. The timid babies cry, arch their backs and flex their limbs in these situations. As toddlers they are frightened of strangers and unfamiliar places, and as four-year-olds they falter and turn to their mothers when told by a psychologist to do something naughty like pour juice on the table. Studies of identical twins — who share exactly the same genetic code — show that genes play a major part in differences in temperament.

It's hello from me ... and from him. How much is temperament down to nature or nurture? Studies with identical twins give some of the answers.

By attaching electrodes to babies' heads and measuring their brain activity, psychologists have found brain differences between timid and bold children. Timid babies show more activity in the right-side of the brain and extrovert babies in the left. Various studies have shown that when mums, dads and teachers are asked separately to rate the child's temperament, they agree only about half of the time.

Some studies have shown broad differences in temperament between babies from different ethnic groups. Working in the United States, for example, in 1974, Freedman found that Chinese-American babies were calmer and easier to soothe when upset than European-American babies. The differences persisted over the first few months and affected the way the babies were treated.

Motor development and learning rush along hand in hand between four and five months. Babies usually start passing things from one hand to another. They also work hard at mastering the art of sitting. Sitting up gives a whole new angle on the world. It may involve both hands for a while as stabilizers, but after a few weeks these will be dispensed with as the baby gets used to being at right angles to his legs. Then his hands will be free to explore the new objects which really begin to fascinate him.

What you can do with your baby

Mirror Mirror On The Wall

Mirrors can be a source of great fun to the four-month-old baby. Making acquaintance with that chap with the receding hairline, seeing his face smile as he smiles, his hands move as he moves, can be more entertaining than watching *Blind Date*. Some babies even appear to become quite shy when faced with their own reflection – a reaction which adults find immensely appealing. Getting the distance right makes all the difference. What the baby sees is effectively twice as far away as the mirror itself, so the mirror should be close enough to keep that image in focus. A distance of about fifteen to nineteen centimetres (six or seven inches) should be right.

To make things more interesting you could try fitting junior out with a hat. Another trick is to creep up behind him so he does not hear or feel your presence. Does he turn round to you? At this stage it is unlikely but in another few months he will have worked out that what he sees in the mirror can tell him what is behind. The same sort of thing can be tried with a dangling toy. Does he reach towards the mirror for it or turn round?

You might like to try your own variation of Michael Lewis's experiment – breaking off a mirror conference for a nosewipe and in the process dabbing the baby's nose with a blob of lipstick. Does he react any differently to the Rudolph look-alike in the mirror? At four months he will not, but if you try the trick again at nine months, twelve months and fifteen months you should be able to see his reaction change as his sense of self develops.

CHAPTER 6

Thinking the Unthinkable?

At five months old babies are beginning to get to grips, mentally, with what goes on around them. They may not be able to show it yet, but it is surprising how much they already know about the world around them.

> The room is dark. His eyes round, five-month-old Leon is intent on the lighted stage in front of him. This is his first-ever puppet show, but it is a puppet show with a difference. On stage he can see one big bouncy Mickey Mouse doll. He smiles, stretches out both his arms to it and watches as the lady who is putting on this special performance moves Mickey behind a screen. She picks up a second Mickey Mouse, shows it to her diminutive audience and he can see her quite clearly adding it to the first one behind the screen. He waits in anticipation. She lifts the screen to reveal... Yes! Two Mickey Mouses (or is it Mickey Mice?). He stretches towards them, beaming his approval. He likes that. But after watching a few repeats he's got the hang of the plot and he's less impressed. His gaze wanders. The lady would say he had 'habituated'. Then a strange thing happens. This time the lady runs through

Getting to grips with how the world works.

the trick as before – one Mickey Mouse, another one added – but when she raises the screen, instead of two, there are three Mickeys on stage! This is clearly a more impressive trick. He stares at them for quite some time... much longer than before. Plainly something does not add up.

Imaginative experiments like these have given scientists a glimpse of how babies even as young as five months already have an idea of how the world works. Here a Mickey Mouse puppet is placed on a stage. The screen comes up to hide it and a second puppet is seen to join the first behind the screen. When the screen is removed there is only one puppet there.

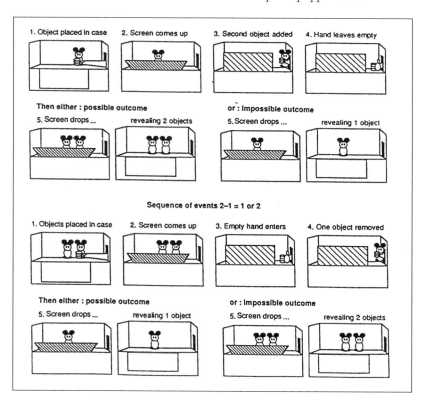

1. Object placed in case   2. Screen comes up   3. Second object added   4. Hand leaves empty

Then either : possible outcome   or : Impossible outcome
5. Screen drops ...   revealing 2 objects   5. Screen drops ...   revealing 1 object

Sequence of events 2–1 = 1 or 2

1. Objects placed in case   2. Screen comes up   3. Empty hand enters   4. One object removed

Then either : possible outcome   or : Impossible outcome
5. Screen drops ...   revealing 1 object   5. Screen drops ...   revealing 2 objects

The idea that babies as young as five or six months can count might be flabbergasting to parents, but over the last few years researchers have come up with more and more evidence that babies – even newborn babies – can tell the difference between two and three objects.

Professor Karen Wynn at the University of Arizona has been doing experiments like the one described and she is among a group of psychologists who strongly suspect that babies are born with a grasp of numbers.

'That is not to say that they are sitting in their cribs thinking to themselves: "Ah, two, what a nice number two is, smaller than three and it seems to be even". Being able to reason about numbers of things that they can see and feel is very different from being able to think about two as an abstract entity,' she says.

In other words she believes the baby's idea of numbers is not an abstract thing – it is very much tied to objects in their world.

It was in the 1980s that the first glimmerings of the 'numerate newborn' were picked up. Researchers working with babies of only two and three days old could demonstrate that, even within hours of joining the world, these infants could tell the difference between one apple and two apples and between two apples and three. What they did was to show them slides of, say, two objects repeatedly, then show three objects, and check to see if the babies looked longer at the new number. In this way they showed quite clearly that well before babies have learned about figures, or even heard the words, they have some idea about numbers ... or at least small numbers.

What happens if the numbers are larger? More studies were done. They showed that bigger numbers really taxed the system. Spotting the difference between three apples and four was much more difficult for babies – many of them could not do it – and between four and five objects was virtually impossible. Why should this be?

Some psychologists, like Professor Wynn, point the finger at the limitations of short-term memory.

'Adults would find a similar problem, and limit, if they were shown a handful of coins and asked how many there were. They might manage three or four, but after that they would probably have to resort to counting to say how many there were.'

Another theory is that babies think of numbers, not as distinct quantities, but as 'blurs' on a mental number line. Numbers are more discrete at the lower end, but blur quickly as they get bigger. Babies can tell the difference between 'a lot' and 'a few', but they are hard pressed to spot the difference between 'a few' and 'a few, plus one' and the difference between 'a lot' and 'a heck of a lot' is like adults trying to tell a trillion from a billion.

The rabbits are moved along a track behind the battlement wall. The short rabbit is hidden even when the screen is at its shortest but the long rabbit can be seen crossing the gap. In the impossible event the long rabbit cannot be seen when crossing the gap. Babies show their surprise at this by watching the impossible event longer.

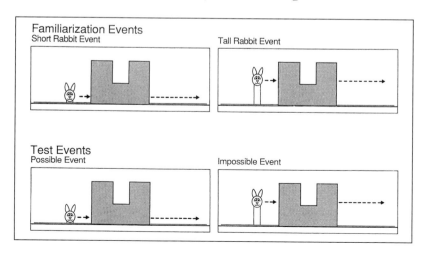

Whatever the workings behind it, the studies showed that babies could tell the difference between one and two. What they did not show, however, was whether babies could count. They could tell two from three, but did they know that two-plus-one equals three? This was what Karen Wynn wanted to establish with her Mickey Mouse experiments – and so she has. With her individual puppet shows she has found that babies – even very young babies – have a grasp of elementary arithmetic. They know one-plus-one equals two, that two-plus-one equals three, and they can do the subtractions too... an ability which she suspects is innate. More, she says: 'From the very first moments babies are actively thinking about their world, reasoning about it and making predictions'.

In other words they are much more active little learners than had previously been thought. Babies are no 'cot potatoes'.

The baby's grasp of basic concepts goes beyond numbers into the realms of everyday physics... a world in which, as adults, we take it for granted that, for example, you cannot go through something solid and that when you drop something it falls down not up. But how do we know these things? Presumably at some stage as babies or toddlers we must have learned them. It would surely be too far-fetched to suppose that we could be born with innate ideas not just about mathematics, but also about physics? Or could it?

A series of enterprising experiments over the last few years in America by psychologist Renée Baillargeon has demonstrated that babies as young as five and six months already notice when things do not seem quite right. Even when their hands-on experience of the world is minimal, they show a grasp of how things should work.

Six month old Alexa has her eyes on a toy car. The lady in the white coat holds it so she can see, then she puts it at the top of a sloping track on a platform in front of the baby chair.

Alexa watches the car roll down, disappear momentarily behind a small screen, come out the other side, and continue down, then along the flat. She laughs and strains forward in her seat.

The lady does it again.

Alexa watches as the car runs down the hill once more.

The lady repeats the performance several times until Alexa is beginning to get restless and look around. Then the lady does something a little different. She lifts the screen so Alexa can see the whole track, then she takes a solid brick and, with Alexa watching, she puts it on the track. Next she lowers the screen so the brick cannot be seen.

Alexa is glued to this pantomime. She watches as the lady picks up the toy car again and puts it on the track at the top of the hill. It runs down just as it did before, behind the screen... and what's this? It's come out the other side as if it's gone straight through the brick.

Alexa stares. Something's wrong here. This is not what she was expecting. The bubble above her head might read: 'I don't believe it!'

Meanwhile, five-month-old Andrew is in his viewing studio watching a screen move like the blade on a waterwheel. It starts by lying flat on the table in front of him, then rotates upwards and through an arc of 180 degrees until it is flat on the table again. He watches this many times until he is quite used to seeing it.

Then the lady appears with a big brick in her hand which she puts down on the table in what would be the path of the rotating screen. It looks like a solid brick. It should be impassable. It should stop the screen from going round.

Andrew then watches as the screen goes all the way round apparently passing through the solid block. He shows his surprise by watching this 'impossible' situation scene for longer than he watches the alternative 'possible' scene in which the screen actually stops at the 120 degree mark.

He, too, registers that this is not how he expects the world to work. Before getting out of his baby chair he has become an elementary armchair physicist!

With simple but arresting demonstrations like these Renée Baillargeon and her colleagues have sparked off an electricity of new thinking about what goes on in young babies' minds... could they be thinking thoughts that we imagined were unthinkable at that age? It is a radical departure from the traditional idea that babies come into the world as blank slates.

For more than thirty years researchers have worked in the shadow of Swiss scientist Jean Piaget. A prodigy himself – Piaget published his first scientific paper, on the albino sparrow, at the age of ten – he believed that the baby's view of the world was radically different from how adults see it. He suggested, for example, that when something disappears from their sight, babies think it has ceased to exist. In other words they have no idea of what psychologists call 'object permanence'. Other 'laws of nature' that we take for granted also have to be learned over time and experience, he said. Probably his single most famous demonstration of this involved pouring water from a short fat glass into a tall thin one and asking a child which glass contains more water. Young children will always say the tall one has more even though they have seen the water being poured from one glass to the other.

It was through close observation of the development of his own three children – Laurent, Lucienne and Jacqueline – coupled with a lifetime's work talking to hundreds of children and giving them puzzles to solve, that Piaget built up his monumental model of how a child's thinking develops. This he described in over forty volumes and 200 articles before he died in 1980 at the age of 84.

He saw the development of thinking in children as a rigid stage-by-stage process in which, for their first two years, babies only learn through their immediate sensations and actions, gradually and laboriously working out for themselves the rules about how the world works. This model has dominated thinking in the field for at least the last thirty years, influencing every figure who has passed this way. The world of academic research, however, revolves around the principle of finding the flaws in previous models, bringing them down and putting up new structures in their place. For as long as his theories have been around, researchers have been seeking the cracks in Piaget's model of how children think, but it is only over the last ten years that Baillargeon and her colleagues have been close to driving in the wedges and really opening them up.

One of the cracks which has attracted team after team of wedge-wielding researchers concerns the most ordinary but baffling of situations. The 'Case of the Hidden Toy' has provided psychologists with a riddle which has kept them arguing for years.

Four-month-old Hannah is sitting on her mother's lap in front of the table. Mum picks up a string of brightly-coloured wooden beads and shows them to the baby. Hannah, delighted with this new toy, immediately reaches for the beads and pulls them to her mouth. After a minute mum takes the beads and, in full view of Hannah, puts them under a cloth on the table in front of them.

The beadless Hannah wails, wriggles, sucks her fingers and looks around at mum, but she does not lift the cloth to get at the beads.

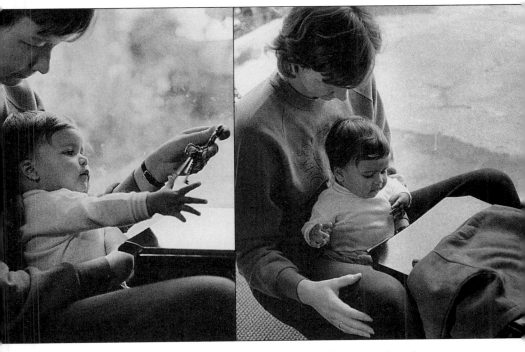

Testing the theory of object permanence — do the keys disappear when they are hidden under the cloth?

In Piaget's view out of sight is out of mind. Hannah has, in psycho-jargon, no idea of object permanence. According to him, for Hannah the beads have ceased to exist, even though she saw them being put under the cloth. Some months later, however, when Hannah is about eight or nine months old, if mum tries the same trick again Hannah will take a different tack. She will spontaneously lean forward and lift the cloth to get at the hidden beads. In the months in between, says Piaget, she has cottoned on to the idea that things can go on existing even though you cannot see them.

This notion that babies see the world as a series of snapshots in which people and things miraculously appear and disappear, unquestioned, has been internationally challenged by psychologists. They have attacked the idea of object permanence with a battery of deviously designed experiments using mirrors, holograms, stereoscopic images and other high-tech appliances. It was in Dundee, however, not far from the offices of the *Beano*, that Peter Willatts and Bruce Hood took the idea back to basics and with little more than a darkened room helped open up a major fissure under this one of Piaget's key concepts.

> Five-month-old Thomas is sitting with his mother behind him, her arms across his chest, preventing him from moving. An intriguing toy hoves into view on his right-hand side, but mum will not let him reach for it. The light goes out. Thomas looks up. The room is completely dark. He cannot see anything, not even the infra-red video system which is filming him. Mum takes her hands away and Thomas immediately stretches out to where he last saw the toy. He obviously does not believe that it has vanished off the face of the earth.

If babies do not think things just disappear when they are hidden, why did Hannah not lift off the cloth to get at her beads? This poser has inspired a virtual snowstorm of academic papers, each trying to explain what was going on in Hannah's baby brain when she let a cloth come between her and the object of her desire. If that problem started a snowstorm, what it led on to – 'The Case of the Muddled Search' – has caused a blizzard. Although it only really becomes apparent in eight-to-nine-month-old babies it is worth looking at here because of the light it might shed on the way problem-solving develops.

Cryptically known among the psychology set as the A-B̃ error (that is, the A not B error) this teaser has both begged and defied explanation since it was first demonstrated sixty years or so ago. Students have written essays on it, academics have presented it at conferences, psychologists have discussed it at seminars and dinner parties, researchers have huddled in laboratories in the UK, Europe, the United States, adjusting this factor, trying that, hypothesising, theorizing, modelling... and still no single explanation has been agreed. Here is the problem:

Eight-month-old Benazir is playing with a bunch of car keys. Her dad takes them and, with her watching, puts them under one of two cloths, Cloth A, on the table in front of her. Benazir is not fooled. Eight months' experience of the world tells her that if she lifts the cloth the keys will be there, waiting. She lifts Cloth A and there they are.

No problem.

Dad plays the same game a couple of times more – always hiding the keys under Cloth A.

Benazir finds them every time. Then dad changes the routine. This time he takes the keys and, as Benazir watches, puts them under Cloth B. Benazir leans forward with a smile and looks for the keys. But what is this? She is looking under Cloth A where she has found them before, not under Cloth B where she saw dad put them!

What is going on here? She knew to look under Cloth A in the first games so she must have an idea that the keys have not ceased to exist. She saw them being put under Cloth B, but still she looked under Cloth A. Why should she do that? Are babies not, after all, the bright sparks we took them for? Piaget had to go through some rather unconvincing mental acrobatics to explain that one. The baby, he said, thinks that she is magically creating the object when she lifts the cloth so she does not see any need to switch to Cloth B. Since then explanations have been offered on a 'pick a card, any card' basis. They have pointed to memory limitations, to the difficulty babies might have of inhibiting impulses, to changes in the way babies search as their brains develop, to sheer force of habit...

The memory argument seemed like a good possibility. If Hannah had built up a memory over several games that the keys were hidden under Cloth A, that memory of Cloth A as the place to search, would be a strong one. If she then saw the keys placed under Cloth B, her memory of Cloth B as the place to search would be brand new, a 'once-off' and relatively fragile. Any delay in looking for the keys could mean the Cloth B memory evaporates in the meantime, but the stronger Cloth A memory remains and so that is where she searches. It seemed like a reasonable idea. It was backed up when experimenters found that holding babies back so their search was delayed did indeed make for more errors of the A-$\tilde{\text{B}}$ variety. Could the riddle have been solved? Was this just a memory problem?

Two plastic cups said no. In the late 1970s George Butterworth did something very simple which got that A-$\tilde{\text{B}}$ debate going all over again.

Hannah is playing the key game once more with dad. But this time instead of having two cloths on the table he has two transparent plastic cups. Just as before he starts by hiding the keys under Cup A several times running. Hannah lifts Cup A to retrieve them. Then he puts the keys under Cup B. She has watched him do it. She can see the keys through the plastic cup.
    What does she do? She leans forward and lifts up Cup A!

So the theorists went back to their arguments whistling 'Thanks for the memory'. What is it all about? Are babies not so bright after all? One of the most appealing explanations comes from Peter Willatts. He suggests that babies are not being dim when they fail in the key search, the difficulty is more an imbalance between what they know, what they can do and the meshing together of these into a strategy to solve the problem.

'The problems that an infant can solve,' Willatts says, 'do not just depend on what they know. They also depend on what skills they have. You could hardly expect a five-month-old who is just learning how to pick up objects, to sort shapes and "post" them in a standard shape sorting toy. Yet surprisingly this obvious fact has been often overlooked by researchers with the result that infants' problem-solving abilities have been under-estimated.'

Put simply, babies may know something at one level, such as 'the keys are under B', but be unable to produce the right act in response to that. In other words they do not act on the WYSIWYG (what you see is what you get) principle.

This mismatch in marrying what you know and what you can do to produce a reasonable strategy to win your heart's desire is possibly also what is seen in another of those simple but startling demonstrations the cognitive psychologists have been so good at surprising us with.

Hannah sits in front of a see-through perspex screen. In front of her there is a hole big enough for her arm to go through. Mum shows her those lovely wooden beads again, but before Hannah can get her hands on them mum has put them behind the screen directly in line with the hole. Hannah leans forward, pushes her hand through and grabs the beads with a delighted smile.

But life is not going to be that simple for Hannah. After being in possession of her treasure for only a moment, she loses the beads to mum who returns them to the other side of the screen. This time instead of being directly behind the hole they are slightly to one side, so to get them Hannah would have to put her arm through and round.

Hannah is baffled. That six-inch diversion might as well be a brick wall. She cannot figure out how to get the beads. Physically there is nothing to stop her. Mentally she knows – she can see – the beads there, but she is unable to put these two things together and claim her prize. Poor Hannah.

In the first problem Hannah could see those keys were under Cup B yet she still tried to find them under Cup A. In the second she could see the beads but could not figure out how to make her arm turn the corner and claim them. Willatts would say the problem lies in bringing together her knowledge and her skills to form a strategy.

Another in-vogue explanation sees these errors as belonging to the same sense of brain disengagement that makes us continue to write the previous year on our cheques well into January of the next year. It is all to do with the frontal cortex. This is the part of the brain – still very immature in the six-month-old – which houses the equivalent of a control tower. A key role of this 'control tower' is to stop things from taking off when the time is not right – in other words to inhibit responses. In the six-month-old baby this part of the brain is relatively underdeveloped but over the first year it matures rapidly ... just as the response to the A-$\tilde{\text{B}}$ search matures. It could be another example of the development of one system – control – lagging behind the development of other systems. When it finally comes up to power it allows the baby to control her impulses and act on the knowledge she has.

More evidence for this explanation comes from a less appealing quarter – frozen monkey brains. It is one of those curious findings which litter the many-roomed house of science, that monkeys, whose brains are at room temperature, do not make A-B̃ errors. Freeze the frontal cortex – in other words switch off their control towers – and those same monkeys make the revealing A-B̃ mistake.

We have seen plenty of evidence in previous chapters that babies are not the empty-handed travellers they were thought to be. They arrive with a certain amount of, as it were, 'head luggage'. It looks as if they are pre-programmed in a variety of ways. Mostly that 'head luggage' helps them in their quest to learn about the world, but maybe sometimes it can hinder. Could the solution to these apparently simple tasks be bedeviled by the way innate thinking mechanisms are themselves developing?

Fascinating Findings

The baby's brain is believed to have all its nerve cells at birth, but not all the connections are made between them. These connections, or synapses, develop as the baby develops, speeding up the brain's processing time as they do so. The adult brain is thought to have about one quadrillion synapses.

Between two and five months babies begin to think much faster. This is particularly noticeable in their habituation times. While newborn babies might take five or ten minutes to get used to something new, by three months they might take 1.5 to 2 minutes and by six months they can do it in thirty seconds.

🎲 Exposure to lead in the atmosphere – a by-product of car exhausts - destroys the fatty myelin which sheaths nerves in much the same way as rubber casing insulates electrical cables. The baby's nerves do not all come ready-sheathed. Myelin is laid down over the first months of the life – a process which helps speed up the brain's processing time.

🎲 Babies as young as five months can recognize a photo of a face they saw two weeks earlier according to research done in the 1970s. Experimenters showed the babies a set of face pictures then several days or weeks later brought them back to the same laboratory where they were shown some of the familiar first faces mixed with some new faces. Using the habituation test the researchers found that the babies looked more at the new faces, thus showing that they remembered the pictures they had seen before.

🎲 Babies of between five and six months can reach out and grab a fast-moving toy! By attaching fluffy rabbits to sticks and driving them past babies at speeds of forty centimetres per second (roughly the speed of a running spider) Audrey Van Der Meer, in Edinburgh, has shown that babies can time and judge their pounce quite accurately – a feat which astonishes their mothers.

What you can do with your baby

Hide and Seek

Young babies react quite differently from adults or even to toddlers
when they see things being hidden under cloths or behind barriers.
When you are five months old if your toy is covered by a cloth –
even if you can still see a part of it – it might just as well be on the
moon it seems. Within a few months, however, something clicks
and babies realize that out of sight is not necessarily out of reach.
Then they will lift cloths and cups to get at the hidden toy. To see
this puzzling reaction in the flesh all you need is a four- or five-
month-old baby, a cloth, or an upside-down cup, and an interesting,
smallish toy like a bunch of coloured keys or beads. First, convince
yourself that your baby is able to grab the cloth or cup. Then, with
the baby sitting in her seat or on a lap in front of the table, show her
the toy. Let her reach for it but, instead of letting her grab it, let her
watch you lift the cloth or cup and hide the toy underneath. What
does she do? Does she try to lift it to get at the toy?

Perhaps she would lift it if she could still see a bit of the toy
sticking out? Try the same trick again but, this time when you hide
the toy, make sure part of it can be seen easily. Does the baby lift the
cloth now?

You could try the trick a third time to convince yourself that
seeing the toy under the cloth or cup does not help the baby solve
the problem. This time use a see-through plastic cup or a piece of
see-through material like net curtain or gauze. The baby can see the
toy, but does she lift the cover to find it?

CHAPTER 7

Early IQ Spotting

'One last push.'

'Waa-waa.'

'Congratulations, Mrs Einstein. It's a boy. He's
eight pounds and he has an IQ of 180!'

How soon can you tell how bright your baby is? Are signs
beginning to show now he is six months old? After all at this age he
is beginning to show more interest in what is going on around
turning his head quickly to familiar voices, examining things for
longer periods, passing things from one hand to another, and
beginning to make sounds of two syllables like 'gaga'. Are these
indications of future IQ?

This is a question many a parent – politically correct in every
other way – would love answered. Mums and dads are always looking
for signs that they might have spawned genius material. That first
smile, first step, first word - is it on time? Is it early? Is my baby
bright? It is, however, the kind of question psychologists hate. They
remind parents that intelligence is not like big ears – a fixed
commodity which babies are born with. They remind them that a

*Examining things for longer periods, passing them from hand to
hand – are these early indications of IQ?*

lot of it – and no one is quite sure how much – depends on environmental factors. Things like stimulation, health, diet, poverty, opportunities for learning, encouragement, even life traumas can have an effect. They remind them that intelligence is not static like having brown eyes. It shifts over life, sometimes quite dramatically. Parents hear all this and go back to their babies chastised... and still looking for signs that they are bright young sparks.

Of more legitimate interest than early signs of genius, as far as child professionals are concerned, and decidedly more politically correct, is the search for early signs of learning difficulties... problems. Brain damage at birth, premature complications, Downs Syndrome, phenylketonuria (PKU) ... there are a host of factors which can mean mental deficiency or difficulties in learning later. Some of these, such as Downs Syndrome and PKU, are easily diagnosed from the start. Others may not become apparent until much later - often when children go to school. By then precious time has been lost.

Children develop at such a rate in those early months and years that the sooner such a diagnosis can be made, the better the chances of being able to do something. Play therapy, exercises, extra opportunities before school all help to bring a child on, and the sooner the remedial work is started the more opportunity there is to develop that child's potential. At present infant tests are poor and of only limited value in picking up babies at risk of learning difficulties later.

This, say the psychologists, is the real justification for measuring babies' intelligence, and exciting discoveries in the last few years in the United States and Britain have brought a new sense of urgency

How soon can you tell how bright your child is? Long before school age there are signs to be read. Psychologists are more interested in picking up those likely to have problems.

to the hunt for the infant IQ test. Psychologists believe they have stumbled on a key which can unlock the secret chamber of intelligence. Now they want to file it down so the key turns that lock every time – and as early as possible. At the cutting edge of this fascinating area of research in the UK, are Peter Willatts in Dundee and Alan Slater in Exeter. Working with babies sometimes only days old, and tracking them through their early childhood, they are hot on the trail of what child experts have long been seeking – a tool which can predict from the earliest months how smart that child is likely to be later.

Up until the early 1980s this area of research had fallen into the doldrums. The trouble was that the tests psychologists were using to score babies' IQs simply did not show much of a relationship with their scores later. The measures tended to concentrate on what psychologists call sensory-motor reactions – things like whether babies turn round when they hear a dog bark, how much attention they pay to a mirror, how they react to a rattle... On the face of it these tests did not seem to tap the information-processing that was going on in babies' brains which we might expect to be linked to intelligence. Children's scores swung wildly from one age to another, and how they scored as babies did not tally closely with how they scored as adults.

The thinkers thought about this, and what they thought was that perhaps there is no such thing as a general intelligence factor in infancy. Perhaps there is no stable core IQ which carries through to childhood and adulthood. That would explain why test results were so inconsistent over the first few years.

Another camp took a different view. They believed there was a stable core IQ but that babies develop mentally in a series of stages. What the early tests pick up, they said, is fluctuations reflecting changes in the stage the baby is at rather than some enduring difference in mental ability. It seemed relatively pointless to psychologists to continue the search for an infant IQ detector. Researchers were not convinced it existed, and even if it did, they suspected it was somehow disguised by the process of development. They turned the research gas down to a peep and went away to fry other fish. Then in the 1980s a series of small studies, mostly in the United States, started to bubble and each one briefly pushed up the lid on infant IQ allowing a tantalizing glimpse of what might be simmering there. What the experimenters were investigating was our old friend habituation (see page 21) and his close associates, visual attention et al.

The habituation technique – simple, cheap and very versatile – has opened window after window on the shadowy world of the baby's mind and allowed a fresh wind of research to sweep through.

By propping up babies in semi-reclining chairs in front of video screens and watching their viewing habits, psychologists have discovered enough to fill books with data on how babies see and think. Show babies a new picture and some will absorb it very quickly. Others look at it for much longer before they have it 'taped'. Could these differences be a reflection of differences in intellectual capacity? Could the ubiquitous habituation test also be the key to measuring infant intelligence?

It seemed a likely candidate. First of all it looked as if the habituation tests were tapping into the brain's information-processing system. When babies look at a new picture the impression is that they are extracting the relevant details from it and stowing them away in the brain. It seemed a more convincing link to intelligence than whether a baby turns round to the sound of a doorbell. Second – and just as important – there was plenty of evidence that habituation tests were sensitive to individual differences between babies. After all there is no point in having a test on which everyone scores much

By propping babies in front of screens and watching their viewing habits scientists have filled books with data on how babies see and think.

the same. Some babies clearly absorbed a new picture, for example, much faster than others. Third – older babies perform faster than younger ones which would be entirely consistent with habituation reflecting IQ.

A number of studies in the USA were certainly pointing in that direction but, because the preoccupation of the researchers was chiefly with diagnosing difficulties, the babies tested tended not to be very representative of the general population. They included many more than usual premature babies or infants at risk in some way. What was needed was a major study in which the babies were a more representative bunch. The trouble with these developmental studies, however, is they take so long. Checking out how an infant's score can predict his or her adult IQ is not a project for the impatient... or the impecunious. It means waiting for the big answers over an entire generation – a long time for any researcher to sit on his hands planning a sequel for his grandchildren. Is there no shortcut?

At the University of Colorado in the late 1980s Lisabeth DiLalla and her colleagues had an idea. Twins. What if, they reasoned, we got round this long-term problem by looking at twins – taking an average of their scores and, while waiting for them to grow up, comparing that with the average IQ of their parents. This 'mean parent IQ' is roughly the IQ they might be expected to show as adults. It was a rough-and-ready idea but it cut out the generation waiting game, and any pointers it gave to habituation and IQ could then be tested in the more widely accepted way – with a long-term study. At the same time it seemed like a good idea to compare the various baby tests in use, to see which worked best.

While his twin, Chip, waited for the second performance, Chuck took his seat on his dad's lap, ready for the matinée. In front of him were two pictures – one on the left and one on the right. He did not notice the peephole between them. While he eyeballed the pin-ups he didn't realize that he too was being given the once-over by a spy between them, recording his every glance, every fixation through the reflections in his eyes. At first the two pictures looked the same then, just as he was getting fed up with the show and wondering whether Chip might be having more fun, one of the pictures changed. This was more interesting. He looked at it for some time. Chuck never knew it but how long he looked at that new face was a matter of huge interest to the spy in the testing chamber.

Using peep-show tactics like these, the Colorado team began testing a squad of over 200 pairs of twins with a battery of measures at seven months, nine months and every year until they were five. Their research verified what the earlier studies had shown – the best predictor of later IQ seemed to come from measures of visual attention. Psychologists would couch it in more careful terms, but the signs were strengthening that babies who learn quickly and then get bored are more likely to be the bright young sparks of tomorrow.

How could these visual attention tests be tapping into IQ? What is going on when Chuck is looking at a new picture? The truth is, no one is quite sure as yet, but psychologists have come up with a battery of processes which could be taking place. They suggest that babies are abstracting information, encoding, categorizing, building up models, memorizing, recalling previous images... all of this in those seconds of habituation. In other words the babies are thinking, and if habituation tests are measuring thinking time it seems reasonable that they should tell us something about intelligence.

So the research is pointing the way forward with habituation tests, but it is not all as straightforward as it seems. Researchers have stumbled on something important to measure, but they are not convinced that they have yet found the best way of measuring it. There are all sorts of habituation procedures and many ways of measuring the processes involved. Some habituation measures are better at predicting childhood IQ scores than others.

Arguments continue over what makes the best test. Some suggest that measuring a baby's preference for a novel picture after only a brief session with a 'familiar' one will do the trick. Others are more inclined to measure how long it takes a baby to habituate to a picture. Still others are examining the baby's pattern of looking. The research has moved on from the question of 'whether' to the question of 'how', and the race is on to develop the best tests. This is the field in which Alan Slater is taking a lead. In a long-term study a batch of Devonshire babies have been tested from their earliest days and will be followed through their pre-school years.

'What we are doing at Exeter,' Slater said, 'is looking at the different ways of measuring habituation and visual attention to compare their predictive value. We are doing a variety of measures of visual attention and then we're testing the same infants at different ages.'

Most researchers began the process in 1992, but the early data is still being analysed and no real results will be known for some time.

Meanwhile at Dundee Peter Willatts and Mary Katherine Dimodugno have already discovered one test with a particularly striking result, and they found it not in the rather artificial experimental set-up we have been looking at, but in a situation much closer to everyday life. Take Chuck out of the viewing chamber, release him from his dad's arms and give him something new to play with. How does he handle a new toy?

Across the ocean, one of Chuck's Dundee contemporaries, nine-month-old Craig has just been handed a yellow plastic train in the cause of science. He grabs it with a chuckle. For him this is fun. He does not realize he and his new train are pushing back the frontiers of research.

He fingers the wheels and tries an exploratory chew on the funnel. While Craig gets to know the chuffer, a team of eagle-eyed researchers, armed with stop-watches, counters and cameras carry out a full surveillance operation.

How long does Craig spend examining the train? What is the sequence of his exploratory behaviour? These, and other questions, keep the researchers amused.

Some babies explore new toys very efficiently. They tend to be the fastest problem solvers. Others are much more disorganised in their approach.

The irreverent outsider might consider measuring not just Craig's habituation time, but the researchers'.

This kind of exploration is what Willatts describes as 'hands-on habituation'. What he has found is that babies who explore new toys very efficiently are also fast problem-solvers at nine months.

'It's a very striking result – a massive correlation,' he says.

Could the way babies examine new toys be a way of predicting intelligence? It is Willatts's hunch that it could. To check this out he and fellow researcher Karen Rosie have commandeered nearly one hundred babies to test and observe periodically from the age of three months through babyhood, toddlerhood and later childhood.

This baby battalion will be put through a variety of hoops as they develop, measuring their habituation – visual and hands-on – how they solve problems and how they perform on IQ tests.

'The study,' Willatts said, 'will tell us if all these infant abilities are related and which is the best predictor of intelligence. If they all predict intelligence the big advantage will be to use the tests at different times to get a broader picture of what a baby can do.'

What worries psychologists is that if there is only one test – habituation – there is more chance of getting it wrong. A slow habituator could be a child who is going to have learning difficulties but, on the other hand, he may be a child having an off day. It will be years before the full picture is filled in, but the first pencillings will be drawn over the next year when results start coming in. Even before then, however, Willatts has evidence to back his hunch. Let us look again at nine-month-old Craig:

Craig has been parted, with difficulty, from the plastic train, but he can still see it. He is sitting on his dad's knee in front of a table and at the far side, out of reach, the train is standing on a piece of cloth. But what's happening now? The man with the white coat has hidden it under a cover.

Craig leans forward, stretching as far as he can, but it's no use. He can't get his hands on that train. But what is this? His flailing hand seemingly hits on the cloth. It moves sideways and the cover on top moves with it. Craig looks at it intently and, almost without a pause, he grabs the cloth with both hands and pulls it inexpertly towards him until the cover comes within his grasp. So far so good. Then he gets hold of the cover and pulls at that. There, underneath, is the train. With a big smile he hugs it to his chest. He has just solved one of life's first problems.

'We have already found that infants who are better at solving this two-step problem,' Willatts says, 'who pull the cloth to get the cover and search under it for the toy, have higher IQs and larger vocabularies at three years.'

Given that babies who examine new toys efficiently also tend to master problems like these faster, it looks as if the case is all but cut and dried.

'We are pretty sure we have now found a second way of measuring infant intelligence as well as habituation,' Willatts, the cautious scientist, added.

This should be demonstrated when Craig comes back at the age of three years for a standard battery of tests designed to rate his IQ. He will be shown pictures of everyday items - of shoes, ships, cabbages and kings, and asked to name as many as he can to gauge the size of his vocabulary. He could also be asked to carry out a series of simple instructions like: 'Pick up the ball, put it in the cup and give it to the teddy'. Strings of commands like these put quite a burden on a three-year-old intellect. To test Craig's memory the experimenter might ask him to repeat a series of numbers like 'five, two, seven'. Each time Craig gets the sequence right, the experimenter will add on another digit until Craig's memory comes up against its limit. These are among the tests designed to tap his IQ at the pre-school stage.

The youngest babies in the Dundee study are three months, but could babies be tested earlier? At Exeter Alan Slater has been measuring the habituation of infants – some only days old – as part of a long-term study tracking them over their first few years. He would not expect tests in those first weeks to yield very reliable pointers of what is to come. One of the problems with testing very young babies is the effect of the birth itself. It can take weeks for babies to get over the trauma of their delivery, and if mum was given painkilling drugs the baby can be affected for a full fortnight afterwards. Launched into the outside world they have only just started to breathe, to feed, to cry and to see. There is so much that is new, and they have a great deal of adjusting to do... perhaps this is not the best time for life's first exam. In addition testing very young babies is an expensive business. They need careful scheduling and they usually require to be taxied to and from the laboratory. Worse, they have a tendency to fall asleep mid-trial! The drop-out rate is sometimes as high as fifty per cent. These problems, however, are not insuperable. Could the time come when parents will know within the first few hours of life how bright their baby will be?

All this pushing back the frontiers can be tiring stuff.

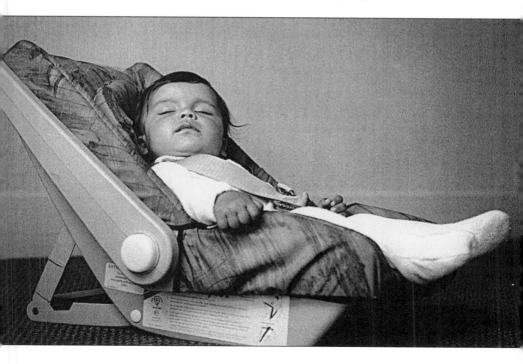

'No,' says Alan Slater. 'We'll never approach that sort of situation. IQ is not entirely genetically determined. There are a whole range of environmental factors which will cause people's IQs to shift up and down.'

He does concede, however, that predictive testing could be feasible by about three months. At-risk babies picked up at that stage could then be singled out for special stimulation – providing as rich an environment as possible.

Just how much environment can affect IQ, even at this age, has been shown by a rash of studies concentrating on that all-important environmental factor – mum. Babies whose mothers talk to them a lot, point things out, and encourage them to pay attention to tractors, balls, fluffy ducks, buses and all the other pop-up features of early life, are likely to turn out to be brighter toddlers. They score better on tests of vocabulary and thinking skills later. It all goes back to that communication link between baby and mother. Once again the evidence is that a good dialogue between the two, oils the wheels of another carriage of developments – this time intellectual. In one particularly impressive case mothers were asked to give their babies a six-month course in what the jargon refers to as 'intensive language stimulation' – they talked more than usual to their babies.

By the time they were a year old the 'hot-housed' babies had spurted ahead putting a massive forty points on their language scores and twenty points on to their general development scores. What does this dramatic finding tell us? It shows that at least part of IQ is remarkably plastic – it can be stretched to quite an extent just by talking. The importance of communication in development is underlined once again. The implications for helping babies – if only their problems could be reliably diagnosed within their first months – is loud and clear.

Even from the earliest weeks, before fast-talking mums have much chance to make an impact, babies show significant differences in how they take in information. Why should this be? Is it some genetic predisposition or is there something else at work?

For ten years they have seen these relationships between habituation measures and IQ scores, and still they are in the dark about what they are actually tapping into. There are two main lines of thought here. The first is that habituation simply measures the speed of processing – in other words, how fast you can think. Picture a city with a slick traffic system – you can get through it quickly and efficiently and get your business done. If, however, the roads are down to single-file traffic and the lights are slow to change the same business can take twice as long to accomplish, if it is ever done at all. That is the idea here – that some babies are born with fast connections, others with slow, and these are more or less fixed for life. Children with fast systems habituate quickly, and consequently can learn quickly. By three years old they will have covered more ground so their performance on the IQ test will be better. Children with slow processing need more time to take in information. As a result they are slow to habituate and by three years old they simply will not have taken in as much as the bright babies.

Alternatively the differences in babies' habituation times could be something more to do with their personal style – how they tackle information-processing. Look around any senior school class and you will see students who sit quietly absorbing lectures, taking neat notes and producing work on time. You will also see others whose attention wanders, whose note-taking is sporadic and whose home-work is messy. Both may have the same potential, but one will learn better because she is more organized in her approach. During his Dundee study Willatts was particularly struck by such differences in the babies' styles.

'Given a new toy,' he said, 'some babies pick it up, turn it round, handle it, play with it and get all their exploration of that new toy over in one or two bouts – those are the children who can solve problems very efficiently. But some are much more disorganized in the way they come at a new toy. They seem to be all over the place. They might look at it, bang it on the table, put it in their mouths and repeat that lots of times as though they couldn't focus their minds on one thing. They are very poor at solving problems. They are the kids we expect to show lower IQs in a couple of years time.'

The star problem-solvers were more organized in the way they explored new toys. They seemed to concentrate all their attention on them, handling, turning round, shaking, and getting the whole business of 'new toy learning' out of the way relatively quickly and efficiently. The slow habituators gave the impression of being disorganized and easily distracted. Could it be that these tests reflect not how fast children think, but how efficiently they can control their thinking and attention?

'It is really important to sort this out,' Willatts said, 'because if intellectual ability is based on how fast the brain functions and that is fairly fixed, there's not much we can really do. But if it's how easily we can control attention, then I think that could be helped.'

So it seems that early IQ spotting is not such a world away after all. Predictive testing could be feasible from about three months old. It is just a question now of refining the tests. It may be that what infant habituation measures show is just one part of the intelligence equation, but that in itself could be a valuable thing to know. We may not be able to spot the Einsteins before they get out of nappies, but if we can spot the slow developers early then we could be opening up windows of opportunity to help. All we need to find out now is what are the best tests? The answers are tantalizingly close.

Fascinating Findings

Between the ages of two-and-a-half years and seventeen, a child's IQ score can shift considerably. An average range of 28.5 IQ points was recorded in one study, with one child in three changing their score by more than thirty points, and one in seven changing by more than forty points.

Children with high IQ scores are likely to show bigger changes in their performance on IQ tests over the years than children with low IQ scores.

Just as children go through physical growth spurts and plateaux, so the rate of their mental growth varies. Big changes in IQ are most likely to occur at the ages of six and ten years.

Children living in rural isolation tend not to score as high on IQ tests as children living in villages and towns. On average rural children come out five points down on their street-wise peers. Some researchers suggest that this is due to the nature of the tests rather than the abilities of the children.

Children who show high IQ scores tend to have parents who talk to them and respond to their feelings. They are also likely to come from homes where there is plenty to capture their attention and imagination – not just toys and play materials but also a variety of experience.

🎲 Homes where the regime is heavy-handed and children are used to punishment, rejection and a mass of rigid rules tend to spawn low achievers.

🎲 Stressful events like a death in the family, parents divorcing, a move and even the birth of a brother or sister can make for dramatic changes in intellectual performance. Scores may, however, recover later – although sometimes it can take several years.

🎲 'Hot cognition' is a term used by psychologists to take into account the all-important emotional side of the intellect – motivation, self concept and feelings about success or failure. Japanese mothers take a much more hands-on role in their children's education than western mothers. They see themselves as 'kyoiku mamas' – education mums – and are actively involved in helping their children achieve academic excellence.

What you can do with your baby

Sharpening Skills

At about six months many babies can pull themselves up to sit if both their hands are held – something they are usually very eager to do. This new vertical position, however, requires a certain balancing skill and for the first few weeks the baby will need both hands to act as stabilisers – planting them either side of himself on the floor in the classic tripod position. Of course this means his hands are not available to reach, grasp and feel the toys which have recently become such a source of interest to him. Within a few weeks he will be able to do without first one, then both of his props and sit 'no hands'. Parents usually like to leave something soft behind their babies at this stage to cushion the occasional fall.

Reaching and grasping are also becoming quite accurate by this time and routines of offering a rusk or ball with a 'ta' help build up this skill. Try presenting the rusk high and low, to one side and to the other, to give him practice in coordination. A 'jungle gym' strung across his cot with toys dangling from it will keep him amused for long spells at this stage and at the same time sharpen up his reaching and grasping abilities.

He will probably also be putting both hands round his bottle now when feeding. Try giving him an elementary problem to solve by handing his bottle to him the wrong way round.

At this stage he will still be holding objects in the whole palm of his hand, but will probably be passing them from one hand to the other. You can encourage this by giving him two toys simultaneously, one to each hand.

When lying on the floor to kick, some babies may discover how to move about by pushing themselves along on their tummies – often backwards at first. There is nothing like a touch of frustration to drive a baby on in his development. Do not be too eager to solve all his problems for him, you could be robbing him of initiative and the satisfaction of succeeding all by himself. You could encourage him to move by putting a toy just out of his reach on the floor. If he is making all the kicking movements and getting nowhere, try putting your hands behind the soles of his feet so he has something to push against – it may be just the encouragement he needs to get himself going.

CHAPTER 8

Getting Moving

Jennifer, aged seven and a half months, is doing her first bungee jump in the cause of science. The experimenter she thought had been so friendly a moment before, is lowering her slowly through the air while an electronic device strapped to her chest records her thudding heart... and Jennifer's heart is certainly thudding. It looks to her as if she is way above the ground and she does not feel too comfortable about it... as her racing heart testifies. Mum makes some reassuring noises but Jennifer knows a drop when she sees one. She is slightly less worried when the drop looks less, but it is a great relief when all the aerobatics come to an end and she can crawl back to mum and complain vociferously.

When it comes to her turn, seven-and-a-half-months-old Dawn, is not upset at all. Dangling over a gaping chasm? It's all in a day's play. Her heart barely registers a flutter whether the drop is deep or shallow...

But then Dawn is at what psychologists like to call the 'pre-locomotive stage'.

Unlike Jennifer she cannot crawl.

The ability to crawl – which often emerges around seven months

Getting moving changes your view of the world.

– brings a whole new perspective to the baby's world. If you have ever become used to being a car passenger on a regular journey then had to take the wheel and drive that journey alone, you will have an inkling of the changes involved. You notice dangerous bends and crossroads, junctions and places where decisions must be made in a way you never did when you were not in the driving seat. Something similar seems to happen with babies. Once they can move around under their own steam they begin to look at things differently... as psychologists such as American Joseph Campos have shown with experiments like the one above.

In fact it is not as bad as it seems. Jennifer is being dangled over what psychologists call the 'visual cliff'. Essentially the 'visual cliff' is two chequered surfaces – one lower than the other – with a sheet of glass over the top. It looks as if there is a huge drop between the shallow and the deep surface, but in fact the glass means there is no difference at all. This arrangement was dreamed up by psychologist Eleanor Gibson over thirty years ago to check whether babies can see depth. Since then it has captured the imagination of a generation of experimenters who have encouraged many a budding Evel Knievel over the edge in the interests of science.

For years it was thought that fear of heights must be innate because when babies were set up to crawl over the visual cliff they were generally afraid of going over the brink. But, of course, the babies were at least six months old and crawling before they could be tested in this way.

Then Joseph Campos had a hunch that how babies reacted to the drop might have more to do with whether or not they had learned to crawl. He wondered whether being able to move around might change how you think about the world. He had heard hair-raising tales from many a mother of fearless babies plunging off tables and sofas while still in the 'L' plates stage of crawling. In

The visual cliff – a sheet of glass over two surfaces, one lower than the other – fools babies into thinking there's a drop.

order to try the 'visual cliff' on pre-crawlers, he had decided to dangle babies over the drop and measure their heart rates.

What he found was that before they could crawl babies did not seem to be afraid of heights, but once they had a little experience of moving themselves around they looked at these drops with a different view... fear.

Next he asked, what if babies could not crawl but had moved

themselves around in baby-walkers – was that enough to colour their view? He tried it out by dangling an assortment of seven-month-olds over the cliff – crawlers and non-crawlers, some of whom had used baby-walkers and some who had not. A clear pattern emerged - immobile babies who had never crawled or been in a baby-walker were unimpressed by the yawning chasm. Babies who had never crawled but who had used baby-walkers did show fear of heights, but babies who crawled and used the walker showed the greatest reaction to the drop. It certainly looked like evidence that moving around, and especially moving around under their own steam, could change the way babies think about the world.

Taking this a stage further scientists have exposed babies to all kinds of terrain – waterbeds and slippery slopes, up and down – to see whether being able to crawl or walk makes you more sensitive to such things. They have found that while walkers are (sensibly) fazed by waterbeds and refuse to go over them on two legs, crawlers take them in their four-legged stride. It seems that, once babies get up on their feet, they quickly learn what makes for tricky walking country. In other words, being able to move opens up different ways of thinking about the world. Similarly walkers, it seems, are more wary of steep slopes.

A 1993 report by Karen Adolph, Marion Eppler and Eleanor Gibson in Child Development noted, after testing babies on slopes: 'In contrast to toddlers most crawlers plunged down slopes head-first and many fell'. They go on: 'This very robust and interesting finding [indicates] infants learn much... between crawling and walk-ing'. Quite so.

More gentle evidence that learning to move around – or 'loco-mote' as psycho jargon has it – could seriously change the way you think came from another kind of experiment which involved revolving babies.

Dawn is sitting in a highchair at one end of a cell-like room. It is one of the dullest rooms imaginable. There are no 'landmarks', no features, no furniture. The walls are green from floor to ceiling; each has a little window... and this is the single remarkable feature of Dawn's cell.

The window to her right is surrounded by flashing lights. After sitting for a moment or two in the highchair, Dawn hears a buzzer and a few seconds afterwards she sees the experimenter's head pop up in the flashing window.

This happens again and very soon Dawn is turning round to the window in expectation as soon as the buzzer goes off. Then just as she is beginning to enjoy herself her highchair is wheeled round through 180 degrees and placed at the other end of the room.

The buzzer buzzes. Where should she look? Should she look to her right? Or should she look to the flashing lights window which is now on her left? Dawn, who has not yet learned to crawl, looks to her right.

She is still using her body as a frame of reference.

What happens when Jennifer – who, remember, can crawl – is put through the same routine? She takes her cues from the room and looks to the window. It seems as if she has learned that using her body as a reference point is not a very efficient way of remembering where things are if that body is crawling round in circles.

Making that first lurch forward changes a baby's relationship with her world. It should not surprise us that it also changes the baby. For the first time she has it within her power to follow her own exploratory instincts. She can check out whatever captures her attention, when it captures her attention. The opportunities for learning really open up. She does not have to wait until mum or dad come to her, she can pursue them and get her own social life going. She can feel more in control. She can go places!

It changes things for parents, too. They have to barricade danger zones, mind where they put their feet, and lock away breakables. But the way they talk to their babies also goes through a subtle change. 'No' and 'don't touch' are phrases which figure much more in conversations. Having a 'locomotive' baby is a new and busy chapter for all concerned.

Not all babies learn to crawl. Estimates vary but around ten per cent of babies do not creep (wriggle on their tummies) or crawl before walking. Some roll their way from place to place, some push themselves backwards − a very frustrating way to travel when you can see what you want straight ahead − some bottom-shuffle. Some ignore all the preliminaries and eventually just step out and walk. Can any of these strategies tell us about how babies are going to develop in the future?

According to one recent finding, the first to walk tend to be crawlers and those who go in for no preliminaries between standing and walking. Bottom-shufflers and creepers tend to follow on later. Is early crawling a sign of a bright baby? Could today's bottom-shuffler be tomorrow's parliamentarian? These kind of questions were being asked by psychologists seventy years ago, but no convincing evidence has emerged of a link with later performance.

One of the pioneers in this area in the 1920s was Arnold Gesell who was the first to see the potential of bringing the new cinematograph techniques from the picture palaces into the psychology laboratories. He filmed babies in motion, then used freeze-frame techniques to dissect movement into its different parts. In this way he could examine in fine detail how babies actually put one hand or one foot in front of the other and moved, and − what seemed to be of the greatest general interest − at what age they did so. The picture these techniques built up seemed to emphasize the role of the developing brain rather than anything in the environment. As the nerves became more mature and the body came under increasing control, so it seemed reaching and grasping, crawling and walking also developed.

Could that development be speeded up in some way? This was the question addressed by Myrtle McGraw. She embarked on a series of unusual experiments – training babies to crawl up and down steeper and steeper slopes; giving one twin, but not the other, roller-skating lessons. She found that practice certainly helped but, once given the opportunity, the babies without the early training caught up rapidly. Special coaching did not seem to greatly advance the time at which babies could do things and, as the others soon caught up, the best advice seemed to be to leave babies to develop in their own time.

It looked as if the main question had been answered and research slowed to a crawl. Since the 1980s, however, psychologists have taken a new interest in how babies learn to control their bodies. McGraw made a come-back, saying she had had second thoughts about the all-importance of the physiological processes – maybe early practice does have a lasting effect. She has since seen the youngsters in her study grow up and believes there was a difference – even as young adults – in the quality of their performance. She suggests that if babies can be caught just as a skill, like crawling, is emerging, and then given plenty of challenges to draw it on, that skill can be expanded.

Luke is just beginning to move forward on his hands and knees. With the McGraw regime in mind his mother dismantles his plastic chute and props the slide up slightly at one end. She imagines a future opening out for him as a mini-Munro bagger.

With smiles, sweet talk and sundry toys she encourages him to crawl up the slope. Every time he reaches the summit she slides him back down and makes his hill climb a little steeper – taking care to make sure the slide is safe.

Before he is through his seventh month Luke can crawl up a seventy-degree incline without crampons!

Others have found that practice at sitting and stepping can push development on, though whether there is any ultimate advantage is still debatable. One group of babies given stepping practice of a few minutes a day from as early as their second week until they were eight weeks old, were found to walk at ten months – a couple of months sooner than a similar group who did not have the stepping practice.

Climb every mountain…Challenging a skill like crawling, just as it is emerging, can expand it further according to some psychologists.

The picture is similar for sitting. In 1988 a little class of six-week-old babies was put through an elementary course in sitting. They were helped to sit up for three minutes every day for seven weeks. After that they sat a test (literally) and showed that they could sit upright for longer than babies who had not done the course. Whether their status as master sitters continues to shine through in adulthood remains to be seen.

There is plenty of evidence from studying babies brought up in different cultures to suggest that different routines can lead to some babies sitting, crawling and walking earlier than others. Generally speaking, children from African cultures tend to sit and walk earlier than Western babies who, in turn, tend to be ahead of babies from the Indian sub-continent. At the extremes are peoples such as the Navaho of North America who carry their babies around strapped to cradle boards. These 'flat-packed' infants have little opportunity throughout their first months to exercise and, not surprisingly, are slow to develop skills such as crawling. The Mali in Africa, on the other hand, put their babies through some strenuous work-out routines from birth – suspending babies by their arms and legs, stretching their muscles and training them in sitting and standing positions. As a result Mali babies are 'body wise' at a much earlier stage than their Western contemporaries.

There is also a difference in average walking ages between cities such as London, Paris and Stockholm. Parisian children seem to take the lead, though why this should be the case still a matter for speculation. Recently the focus was on Jamaican mothers living in England. They expect their infants to sit and to walk alone earlier than English mothers do, and they routinely handle their babies in ways likely to help them along that route. As a result their babies did seem to oblige – sitting and walking, according to one recent study, as much as two months earlier than their English neighbours.

On the other hand both English and Jamaican babies crawled at about the same time. Crawling is not something the Jamaicans look for, or have a routine for, in their babies. In fact a massive twenty-five per cent of Jamaican babies in this study never crawled at all. Interesting as these variations are, they are swamped by individual differences between children – even children living next door to each other. It could be that much of the variation is simply due to different opportunities for practice.

Most recently, in 1993, the season at which a baby is born was shown to affect when they learn to crawl. Janette Benson at the University of Denver found that babies born in summer crawl three weeks later on average than those born in winter. She put this down to the fact that summer babies are just reaching the six-to-eight-month stage when poor weather and shorter daylight hours curtail their opportunities to move around. Jackets and warm winter suits could also restrict them, whereas winter-born babies who are ready to crawl during the summer months are likely to be lightly dressed and have more opportunities for action.

The European approach to helping babies to move early is to provide them with their own set of wheels – the baby-walker. It may seem like something invented by Mothercare, but in fact the baby-walker has been around for a very long time – at least since the boyhood days of Oliver Cromwell. Convenient as they have been to mothers down the ages there is no evidence that baby-walkers actually help babies learn to crawl or walk. Quite the reverse, according to some, and accidents involving these four-wheel drive runabouts are common enough for research agencies in the United States to have banned further projects involving them.

To see whether baby-walkers help babies walk or crawl early a 1986 study in London followed over sixty inner-city babies, most of whom had been users since they were around five or six months old. While they found that baby-walkers generally did not seem to affect the age at which babies sat or walked alone, there was a big difference in crawling. Users tended to crawl much later – on average two months later – than non-users. So, far from helping babies learn to move under their own steam, it seems baby-walkers might even slow them down, at least as far as crawling is concerned. In one particularly extreme case a baby, who had spent virtually all her waking hours in either a baby-walker or a baby-bouncer from the age of three weeks, did not learn to sit up until she was over a year old.

> Dawn is in pre-crawling mode, and frustrated. After lying around watching the world go by, she is doing her best to join it. She has managed to lift up her bottom and push up with both hands to achieve the starting position on all fours, but having got there she seems to be stuck. All four limbs seem to be anchored to the floor holding her weight off the ground.
>
> How can she possibly move? She rocks back and forward unable, or unsure what to do next. Mum does what mums have always done. She puts Dawn's most currently desirable toy – a very chewable rubber hippopotamus – just out of reach.
>
> Dawn looks at it. She rocks. She pushes with her hands and is furious to find herself moving further from, not closer to, her hippo friend. She makes a very frustrated 'dididi' sound then reaches forward for the toy with both hands.
>
> The inevitable happens. She collapses on the floor and takes failure on the chin.

The question is how do babies move from this rocking stage to the point of putting their best hand forward? According to some of the latest research, it all has to do with the development of right- or left-handedness.

In 1989 Eugene Goldfield at Connecticut College decided to put crawling under the microscope. He filmed a squad of babies every week from six months old until they crawled, then carefully analysed the sequence of their movements. He looked at how they held their heads, how they kicked their legs, how they used their hands – all elements in the crawling equation. In addition he wanted to know whether they had developed a preference for using either hand – something which many, but by no means all, babies begin to show at around this age. By holding a toy at a centre point straight in front of the babies he judged whether they were right- or left-handed.

What he found was that as a strong hand preference emerged, so babies moved from the rocking to the crawling stage. It was as if regularly reaching for things with one hand made it easier for babies to put their best hand forward when poised to crawl.

This emergence of right- or left-handedness is not a completely straightforward process in babies. The hand they prefer to use at six months may not be the hand they prefer to use at nine months. In fact while ninety per cent of adults are right-handed, the figure is much less – some say fifty-to-seventy per cent – for babies. A number must obviously make a switch from using their left hands to using their rights at some point – usually before the age of two years.

In adults the best test of right- or left-handedness lies in the humble matchbox. If you are right-handed you hold the box in your left and strike the match with your right. Similarly for babies the best test, once they are able to use two hands in a coordinated way, is to give him or her something which needs one hand to hold it and another to do something more demanding. A pot with a lid which comes off is ideal.

The development of 'handedness' in babies is thought to be an important milestone in the development of the brain. The hunch is that as a hand preference emerges so the two hemispheres of the brain could be becoming more specialized. The left hemisphere, which controls the right hand, is the main language processor and it is interesting that at around the time when babies often begin to show hand preference they are also beginning to babble.

These are all hints that the brain of the seven-month-old is beginning to organize itself into a more efficient machine which, as it grows, splits into departments specializing in different areas, each with its own crack team being trained up to handle it. Sounds coming in? Send them to the language department for processing – it will instruct the mouth, tongue and vocal cord team how to respond. Something needing picking up? Tell the right hand – it is the best we've got for the job. But at seven months, even the best hand at the job, has a great deal of fine tuning to do as parents see all too well when it comes to using a spoon.

Dawn, at seven months, has been eating mushy food for some weeks now. She loves the cooking – no complaints about that but the service... Well! What's so frustrating is the hands-off way the food is presented to her – on a spoon held by mum. What Dawn has been trying to tell mum for some time, with a mixture of semaphore and shouted syllables, is that she would like to get her hands on her own cutlery. At last mum, tired of trying to steer the loaded spoon to Dawn's mouth past a pair of flailing arms and grasping hands on the path, gets the message. She gives up and hands her daughter the spoon. Dawn grabs it with a grip more suited to a tennis racket, splatters the dish-of-the-day up the wall and directs the empty spoon into her left ear.

Clearly there is more to this spooning business than meets the eye... er, ear.

That is a view certainly endorsed by Sheffield University researchers Professor Kevin Connolly and Mary Dalgleish who recently published an in-depth study on using spoons. For six months they filmed babies' mealtimes and watched their progress from rough apprentices to cutlery, to smooth(ish) spoon operators. They analyzed the task into a sequence of problems each of which have to be solved – holding the spoon, directing it into the food, loading it up, carrying the food on the spoon (the right way up), finding the open mouth, emptying the spoon and extracting it. In a nineteen-page report they examined grip patterns and trajectories, spoon orientation and anticipatory mouth opening. They talked about visual monitoring, activities of the contralateral hand and the temporal structure of the task... in short, they left readers wondering how babies ever manage to master such an incredibly complex task.

'It is extraordinary when you begin to analyse something as basic as taking a spoonful of dinner what skills are actually involved,' Professor Connolly says. 'The thing about a skill like using a spoon is that it demands such flexibility. You're not going to be a very skilled user if you can only use a teaspoon. You've got to be able to use a soup spoon, too. And how you use it has got to change with things like what you eat - whether you're trying to spoon consommé or Scotch broth, what level of food there is in the bowl, the shape of the dish...'

As adults that flexibility is automatic, but infants have to learn these things and some of them, according to Professor Connolly, can probably be learned simply from being handed a spoon to hold while mum does the real spooning business.

How babies use their hands – and especially how babies hold and pick up things – has been the focus of an explosion of interest in the last few years. Previously the emphasis was on the way their grasp became more refined as their brains developed and matured.

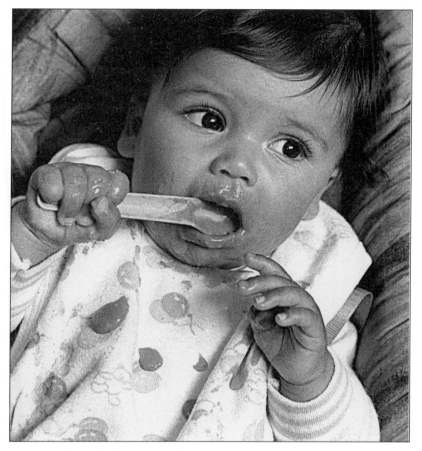

There's clearly more to this spoon-feeding business than meets the eye... er, ear.

Not much attention was given to outside factors. A four-month-old would be expected to grasp things in the centre of the palm of the hand, with all fingers. By seven months the thumb would be expected to come into play, first in opposition to several fingers and later against the index finger.

The latest research, however, suggests things are more flexible — that the environment plays more of a part than was thought, and babies are actually operating at a much more skilled level than had been credited. When they pick things up, for example, they are sensitive to the size and shape of what they are handling. Building bricks — such as those customarily used on early development tests — are picked up in a much more crude way than, say, raisins. The surface on which the objects are sitting is also something babies take into account. If a raisin is sitting on a foam sheet they will pick it up in a different way than if it was sitting on a solid table top. In other words babies are using cues from the world to make decisions about how to behave.

At the same time as all this interest in getting moving, controlling the body and adjusting to the environment is taking place, babies' brains are developing rapidly — particularly the frontal cortex. This area too has been closely associated with emotions — something which begins to take on a more prominent role in the baby's life, as we are about to see.

Fascinating Findings

Do bright babies walk early? Numerous studies over the years have tested the idea that babies who are quick to reach major milestones like sitting, standing, crawling, walking and stacking bricks will go on to show high intelligence later. But they have consistently failed to show any evidence that this is the case. Some highly intelligent children never learn to crawl at all.

🎲 Paediatricians can tell how long a child has been able to sit up by looking at her. If her arms are still being used as anchors either side and she cannot swivel or lean without falling over she is still a novice sitter. If, however, she can swivel round and lean to each side she will have been sitting for at least a month. If she can sit up from lying flat she will have been sitting for at least two months.

🎲 At seven months or so, babies are able to stand while holding on to a support. Within a couple of months they will have mastered the art of pulling themselves into a standing position and at about ten or eleven months they will be standing alone. In the West babies tend to use furniture to help them get up on their feet, but in some countries such as Bali families build special walking rails at the baby's chest height to help mobilise their offspring.

🎲 Babies of seven months – an age at which they do not step forward with their feet under normal circumstances – will put one foot in front of the other when on a treadmill! One research team found that babies of this age could even adjust their walking speed when the treadmill moved at different rates for each leg!

🎲 Between birth and adulthood the human head doubles in length, the trunk triples, the arms quadruple, and the legs become five times as big.

🎲 Recent research suggests that the two hemispheres of the brain are involved in expressing different kinds of emotion. The left-hand side is involved in expressing positive feelings and the right-hand side in negative feelings.

One of the major developments, as far as hands are concerned, is the separation of the forefinger and thumb which begins to happen around seven months. Once the fingers can be operated independently rather than like a rake, babies can pick up small things and manipulate in a much more skilful way. As this skill develops they show more and more interest in using their hands to

The grip becomes progressively more refined from a full hand grab to a controlled pincer movement.

Daycare decisions

As maternity leave ends, the question of daycare arises for many families in which both partners wish to continue to work outside the home. Making the decision to leave your baby in the care of someone else is rarely easy. Parents, naturally, ask the question: 'Is daycare bad for children?' Psychologists, equally naturally, answer that it is not as simple as that. It depends on the quality of the daycare, the age of the child, the number of hours involved, the nature of the home...

The question is an emotive one and research has thrown up confusing and inconsistent results. One of the most influential studies in the 1980s – that of American Jay Belsky – concluded that babies of under a year who spent more than twenty hours a week in day care, had a heightened risk of insecure attachment to their parents. In Sweden, however, one researcher found that babies who went into daycare before their first birthday did better on teacher ratings and tests than those looked after at home.

One of the UK's leading authorities on the subject, psychologist and father of five, Professor Edward Melhuish, has a wealth of practical personal experience to draw on as well as years of research looking into the effects of daycare on babies:

'As parents my wife and I have used all kinds of daycare with our children at different stages. I have stayed home as house-husband while my wife, a nurse, worked shifts. We have also used childminders, nurseries, playgroups, relatives, neighbours... even our teenage daughter who looked after the youngest baby for a spell.'

Overleaf Professor Melhuish answers the questions mostly asked by parents considering daycare for their babies:

What should you look for when choosing daycare for your baby?
• **One-to-one attention** and plenty of it. The attention should be affectionate, responsive and enjoyed by the caregiver.
• **Stability.** Chopping and changing caregivers every few weeks is unsettling for babies. If you are considering a nursery ask if they appoint a key person to look after each child regularly.
• **Experience/training.** The Nursery Nurse Examination Board (NNEB) qualification is evidence of a good basic knowledge of child development. But there are many untrained childminders whose experience can make them excellent for the job. Childminders should, by law, be registered with local authorities who carry out routine checks for safety, hygiene and suitability.
• **Knowledge of the childminder** – either from personal experience of friends. Does she play with the babies in her care? Is she reliable?
• **Safety** – stairs, fires, windows, ponds, streets, snappy dogs – are these carefully kept out of bounds or could they be a hazard?

How can you judge how a caregiver is going to interact with your baby?
• Firstly you can look at the other children. Are they happy? Do they look morose or under-stimulated? Probably the best idea is to stay with your baby for the first session or two. Most people can 'act up' for twenty or thirty minutes but, after that, they tend to reveal their usual pattern of behaviour. Also keep an eye on how your baby reacts when you go to collect him. He may well show some separation anxiety at first, but should have settled down within two or three sessions.

Is individual or group care best for babies?

• For babies, individual care is more likely to offer the amount of one-to-one interaction you want. Later, from eighteen months to two years, group care comes into its own when children benefit from playing with other children. However, if you are looking at a nursery setting for a baby, you should look for a nursery adapted to the needs of babies – in particular a staff/baby ratio of at least one-to-three. As soon as you go above that the carer tends to become so wrapped up in routine caretaking that there is little chance to interact with the babies.

How many hours a week is it 'safe' to leave my baby in daycare?

• There is no magic number of hours that it is safe to work. Most mothers do not have much choice. Belsky's findings that babies who spend longer than twenty hours per week in care suffer developmentally, relate to the United States where daycare is very poor on the whole. I suspect those babies, who were in daycare for long spells – often fifty hours, were not getting enough of that responsive one-to-one attention that is so important. However it is generally suggested that part-time is better than full-time. We have studied 400 families in London and found that those mothers who work part-time enjoy their work and parenting roles more.

What do you think of the idea of 'quality time'?

• I think there is something in it. Basically quality time is this important one-to-one attention we have talked about. Certainly children need a good bit of quality time with whatever caregiver. Given that a working parent might be with his or her child for three or four waking hours per day, at least one hour should be spent in fairly intense interaction.

CHAPTER 9

Don't Talk to Strangers

It is a big day for Sanjay's household. The eight-month-old doesn't know it, but today he is going on his first blind date. His far-flung Granny is due to fly in from foreign parts to meet her grandson for the very first time. So far she has been doting at a distance. Now she can't wait to be a hands-on grandmother.

Mum and dad are equally eager to show Sanjay off. They've dressed him up in a fetching new outfit with little trainer boots to match. They've made sure he has had a good nap so he'll be in excellent spirits. They've even put a little dreadlock in his hair.

Granny sails into the airport lounge her arms open wide. Brushing aside mum and dad's greetings she sweeps Sanjay from his mother's arms, sticks her smiling face into his, and before he knows what's happening she has landed a noisy kiss right on his nose.

He opens his eyes wide and thrusts out his arms and legs in surprise.

'Isn't he just go-ooorgeous!' enthuses granny to the airport at large.

It's a rhetorical question but Sanjay replies anyway in the only way he knows how – a high-decibel 'Waaaa'.

When the unfamiliar rears its strange head, the first reaction may be to burst into tears.

By eight months most babies are beginning to shed their blanket trust in all things two-legged and sociable. Suddenly they become more wary about who they fraternize with. Gone is that affable 'smile and the world will smile with you' attitude. The eight-month-old is becoming more 'cot-wise'. He cries if he is left with strangers. He has his social circle and he has learned roughly what to expect from them. When the unfamiliar rears its strange head he is at a loss. His first reaction may be to burst into tears. It is a reaction that often takes parents by surprise. Up until now they have been able to introduce their baby to friends and relatives, confident that he will give them a friendly reception. Now they wonder what is suddenly causing this alarm? Is it something particular about the strangers and how they introduce themselves? Or is it something within the baby?

Suddenly they become more wary about who they fraternize with...

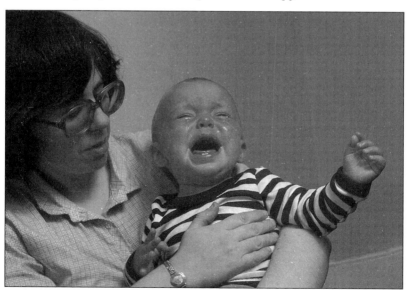

These are questions psychologists, too, have wrestled with. They noted that fear of strangers begins at about the same time that babies are making a surge in development. They noted that at about the time babies begin to show signs of attachment and affection for those closest to them, they also begin, shortly after, to show fear of strangers, and start getting upset at being separated from mum or their closest contact.

All this pointed to some developmental process unfolding within the baby, and, until recently, this fear of strangers was believed to be one of those inevitable stages a baby had to go through, like teething. Whether they were brought up among palm trees or pavements it was widely believed that fear of strangers, from about eight months or so, was just a fact of baby life. In the last few years, however, researchers have shown that this is not quite the full picture. While many babies of this age are afraid of strangers it is not universal and it is not inevitable. The suggestion is, then, that while a good part of this reaction may be due to the way all babies' minds develop, there could also be some outside cues that scare them more than others.

Imagine if, as you are reading this book, a stranger knocked on your door bearing an empty coffee jar and a sexy 'May I borrow?' smile. How would you react? Probably in a friendly way. Now consider how differently you might respond if he was wielding a bloodied scythe and a crazed grin... Are we, as adults, just sensitive that way? Or do babies also pick up cues that make some strangers seem more frightening than others?

Sanjay's grandmother is still licking her wounds from the less-than-rapturous reception she received from her grandson at the airport. Her daughter-in-law reassures her that it is nothing personal — Sanjay is like that with people he doesn't know at the moment. So when a complete stranger – a seven-year-old-boy – comes in for a few minutes to wait for his parents granny is extremely upset to find he is an instant hit with her grandson.

Sanjay smiles and coos at him at once, reaching out to him invitingly with both hands.

'What's he got that granny hasn't?' she demands. 'Waaa,' replies Sanjay which, loosely translated, means 'youth'.

This common observation that babies are more friendly and relaxed towards strange children than strange adults was examined more carefully in an inspired if slightly offbeat experiment by Jeanne Brooks and Michael Lewis. Previously researchers had found that tall strangers, especially tall strangers looming up close to the face, were particularly frightening. Could size be the key to babies' fear of strangers?

To test this Brooks and Lewis engaged a cast of assorted 'strangers' including children, adults and a midget. The idea of the midget was that she combined the size of a child with the looks of an adult. How did the babies react? Broadly, they were friendly towards the children, frightened by the adults and seemingly baffled by the midget. They did not treat the midget as either an adult or a child, but watched her very intently as if they were not sure how to react. So size alone is not the cue.

Various other factors have been explored. Babies have been tested with men and women, with masked strangers and robots, at home and in unusual settings, with and without control of what the stranger does.

Sanjay's grandmother has brought him a present. She just knows 'he's going to lu-uuurv it!'

Sanjay's mother has her doubts, but she allows herself to be swept along by the full flood of grandmother's enthusiasm. It's clear granny aims to claim her place in her grandson's affections and, to help her do it, she has brought him a toy monkey. But this isn't just any boring, stuffed, sit-on-the-bed toy. This is a monkey with 'attitude'.

'Let's give Sanjay a surprise!' says granny, tucking herself behind the curtains. In the middle of the floor the monkey – a brass cymbal in each hand – lies in wait for Sanjay. When the unsuspecting eight-month-old appears on all fours, a delighted granny presses the remote control button and the monkey bursts into an orgy of cymbal-bashing. Sanjay is surprised all right – surprised out of his wits. And he expresses it with a full-volume 'Waaa'.

Granny's getting-to-know-you visit is not turning out to be the success she had hoped.

Perhaps it is the unexpected element that is the main problem? What if Sanjay felt he had more influence over what was going on and the pace it was taking – would he be more relaxed? Using a situation like this Megan Gunnar at the University of Minnesota exposed over sixty babies of between six-and-twelve-months to the cymbal-bashing monkey. Some could predict when it was going to burst into action because they heard a warning bell. Others could control the monkey by hitting a panel. A third group could neither predict nor control the one-monkey-band. She found that being able to predict the scary event was actually more upsetting, at least for girls. They would hear the bell and begin to cry in anticipation. Being able to switch the monkey off and on did help babies keep their fears in check, but only once they were about twelve months old. So control helps, especially in older babies.

With this kind of study in mind psychologists would advise granny to try a different tack if she wants to make friends with Sanjay. They would suggest approaching him more slowly and more sensitively, perhaps even to refrain from looking him in the eye until he had the chance to give her the 'once over'. Their advice would be to smile and sweet-talk her way to a response, then to wait for Sanjay's permission before moving in really close.

These are some of the external factors involved in babies' fear of strangers, but what about the internal ones? What about the baby's relationship with mum, or dad? That seems to have been at the core of so many aspects of development so far, could it also be involved here? How babies react to strange situations has been the subject of a huge amount of study over the last twenty years. This is not just because babies' reactions to strangers is fascinating in itself, but because of its value in throwing light on the relationships babies have with their parents – what psychologists refer to as 'attachment'.

The belief that the way babies relate to their mothers lies at the heart of much of their later development and particularly their relationships on into adulthood has kept psychoanalysts by the couch since the days of Freud.

John Bowlby, one of the most influential men in moulding current views of child development, suggests that the roots of attachment lie in the way mum cares for the needs of the baby. Reactions to signs such as smiling, crying, sucking and so on are, he claims, biologically pre-programmed but in carrying them through mum and baby are brought into plenty of close contact and out of this grows their relationship – their attachment. It was something that everyone knew existed and believed was important, but how could they measure it? It seemed like trying to calibrate the taste of honey.

Then in the 1970s along came a Canadian psychologist with a disarmingly simple idea. Mary Ainsworth, a researcher who had been research assistant to John Bowlby in the 1950s, and then worked extensively with children in Uganda before settling in the USA, strung together a sequence of events which has given a clearer window than mountains of research papers on how babies relate to their parents. She and her team had been closely studying a score of families in their own homes in Baltimore, watching how the mothers fed, held, smiled and talked with their babies – not in a laboratory situation but in real life. They watched the babies too – how they explored, how cuddly they were, how they reacted if mum left the room... and in this way they built up a picture of the styles of the parents and the security of the babies. But Ainsworth had a hunch that the security of the babies would be thrown into much sharper relief if they were in a strange environment.

What she did was to engineer a situation in which babies are left in an unfamiliar playroom full of toys, alone, and with a stranger for a few minutes before being reunited with mum. The testing episode, known as the 'strange situation', lasts only twenty minutes and the crucial measurements are based on only a few minutes within that time. The results, however, have been so illuminating that the impact of the 'strange situation' on modern psychology has been immense.

The crucial question is what does the baby do on reunion with mum? Does he welcome her back? Does he ignore her? Does he put his arms out then push her away when she tries to cuddle him? Or is his behaviour puzzling and disorganized? It is this tell-tale reaction which seems to give a thumbprint of the baby's most important relationship – his attachment to the person caring for him. So widely accepted is the 'strange situation' as a yardstick of attachment that American courts have sought to use it in custody cases. The interesting thing is that this characteristic thumbprint can be seen again and again in different areas of that child's later life.

Those few minutes of seeking reassurance — or not, as the case may be — seem to say more about how things are inside that baby — that person — than any other test.

Using the way they react in the strange situation, Ainsworth classed babies as securely or insecurely attached.

Holly is securely attached. When mum comes back at the end of the session Holly is pleased and crawls to her for a cuddle. Once comforted she crawls away quite happily and goes on playing with the toys on the floor. She is the kind of baby who is comfortable in most situations. She knows she can count on mum being available to her. She is interested in the stranger and in the new toys, and she uses mum as a safe base from which to explore, returning to her after brief forays, to refuel on confidence and security. The majority of children (fifty to sixty per cent) are like Holly.

Then there are the babies like William, Wayne and Tracey who would be labelled 'insecurely attached'. This is where the picture ceases to be stark black and white, and takes on various shades of grey. While there is only one type of secure attachment, it seems babies can be 'insecurely attached' in a variety of ways.

William avoids mum when she returns. He glances away when she looks at him and ignores her invitation to climb up on to her knee. He seems to have learned that the best way of coping with distress is on his own — that mum is not likely to be there for him or perhaps not even helpful.

Better the arms you know...

The crucial question is — what does the baby do on reunion?
Does he welcome mum back or does he ignore her?

He, and the twenty-five per cent of babies like him, are usually less upset by the strange situation. In fact they seem to be quite self contained. Some studies have found that babies who have spent long periods in daycare from an early age are more likely to react this way, though whether this is a reflection of their relationship with mum or because they are more used to strangers is a point of debate.

Wayne has a much more difficult time. He is very upset by the strange situation. But when mum comes back he shows a strange mixture of contradictory emotions. He goes to her for comfort, but when she tries to cuddle him he pushes her away crying angrily.

One in ten babies are what psychologists call 'resistantly attached' like Wayne. These babies need comforting and they seem to expect that their protests have to be loud and angry before they will be heard... and even then they cannot count on mum being helpful.

> Tracey is one of a fourth and very small group of babies only recently identified. She is one who would set alarm bells ringing with childcare professionals. Her reactions are so chaotic it is difficult to draw any coherent pattern from them.
> On mum's return she might cover her face, or freeze, or even lie face down on the floor. It is as if she does not know how best to behave–... as if she is frightened of mum. She is among the 'insecurely attached and disorganized' group.

All this is gleaned from a few seconds of behaviour. And this is the main criticism of the strange situation test – that it pivots on such a brief glimpse of what must be a wider picture. The fact is, that study after study has shown that, in the absence of major life dramas like death and divorce, these patterns of attachment are stable. Re-testing the same babies much later as toddlers and children gives similar results. More, it seems that there are links between how babies react in the strange situation and how they behave in all sorts of other situations – how, as children, they get on with people, how they solve problems, how enthusiastic they are, how persistent, how prone to difficult behaviour... Could their early attachment affect all of these? Whatever it is the strange situation measures it appears to be something which is at the core of how people tick.

Perhaps most interesting of all, a pattern has recently been high-lighted between the generations. How adults feel about their own parents is linked to how their children act in the strange situation... and this can now be shown in measurable, black and white terms.

'That is not to say that if you had a poor relationship with your parents you are destined to repeat that with your own children,' according to university lecturers Howard and Miriam Steele. Based at University College London and the Anna Freud Centre, the Steeles lead a team of researchers who have been tracking the lives and relationships of a hundred families in the capital over the last seven years.

The London Parent-Child Project started in 1987 when the volunteer mothers were all expecting their first babies. Since then the mums, dads and children have been observed and interviewed, questioned and tested in an effort to study ways in which the relationships the adults had with their parents when they were young may have influenced how they relate to their children. Broadly their findings are that those who have come to terms with their own childhood and parents, are more likely to have a secure relationship with their own babies. Those who are still angry, upset and emotional about how they were treated, or who simply refuse to think, or talk, about it will probably not relate well to their own children.

Interestingly this is not necessarily the same as reporting a happy or unhappy childhood. Very few adults (roughly fifteen per cent in this study) seem to follow a simple, uncomplicated route from secure childhood to adulthood. By far the majority, even of well-adjusted adults, report unhappy childhood experiences of one kind or another. In about a third of cases these were serious traumas such as abuse or loss of a parent. What sets these adults apart, however, is that they have come to terms with their past. They show some understanding, even forgiveness of the parents who mistreated them.

In interviews about their childhoods these well-adjusted adults typically give detailed, coherent accounts of their early lives. They remember childhood well and without rose-tinted spectacles. They talk freely about their experiences good and bad, and accept the imperfections of both themselves and their parents.

In contrast some adults are dismissive when asked about their childhoods. They have little to say and they seem to want to deny the significance of their early experience. Sometimes they present an idealized picture of their parents or, when they talk about the bad times, they talk about the facts, with the feelings leeched out. They have been rejected in some way by their parents but they find it hard to tell how this might affect them. These are the adults whose babies tend to be insecure. When tested in the 'strange situation' the chances are, these babies will avoid mum on reunion.

A third group of adults, when interviewed, are still preoccupied with their childhoods. They talk about their experiences in a confused, rambling, sometimes angry and often incoherent way. Their parents, it seems, were lacking in love but not necessarily rejecting. It is clear they have not sorted out the conflicts from that part of their lives. These adults seem to have great difficulty relating to their children in a straightforward way and, as a result their babies do not know what to expect from them. In the 'strange situation' their babies are those who are often most distressed. They cry or whine, seek comfort and then resist it when it is offered.

So we can see that some pattern to do with the relationships between parents and children crosses the generations. The question is, how?

The thumbprint of how babies relate to their parents is already visible when they are eight or nine months old. In that first few months they have already absorbed whatever it is that sets the broad-brush pattern for their relationships later in life. Where does that thumbprint come from? How much is due to mum? How much to dad? What is it that parents do that makes such a difference to their children?

To answer the first question – since they are unable to take a baby's mind to pieces and show the bits that make up attachment – psychologists have had to resort to their usual pastime: building models and theorizing. What they suggest is that babies build inside their minds models of their parents and of themselves, based on their experiences. So a baby who finds mum or dad is comforting, loving and always there when needed, will think of his parents as loving and also of himself as worthy of love. Later when that child has grown he will draw on those models to fulfil his own role as parent in the way he has learned. If, however, he learns early that mum pushes him away or leaves him to cope on his own, not only will his model of her be 'rejecting', but also his image of himself will be of someone not worthy of love.

The theorists suggest that these ideas are already constructed in the first months of a child's life, but, being working models, they can change with life's experiences. This would account for the many adults who report difficult relationships with their parents in their own childhood, but who come to terms with that and go on to develop secure bonds with their own children. For many it seems, all they need is a good attachment figure later – a grandparent, an aunt, uncle, teacher, youth club leader, friend – someone who is there for them.

This gives a glimpse of how the thumbprint is passed from one generation to another. Now who makes it? Is it mum or dad or both? Who has the biggest influence on the baby? It seems from a number of studies now that mums are the main transmitter across the generations. How mums feel about their parents and childhood, ties in much more closely with how secure their babies are compared with how dads feel about their early past.

Some hints are beginning to emerge from recent studies that the kind of relationships babies form with their mothers may be quite different from those they form with their fathers. There is some work to suggest that the mother–child relationship is most important in developing the child's sense of autonomy, competence and persistence. Children who have a good relationship with mum concentrate better in their early years and are more resilient. How a child gets along with dad, on the other hand, seems to set the scene for how sociable he will be and how easily he will make friends outside the family.

So we have seen how the thumbprint is left – how the baby builds up a sense of himself and those close to him. We have seen that mum is probably responsible for more of the thumbprint than dad. What is it then the parents do, or not do, which gives the thumbprint its individual lines?

Mary Ainsworth's work, relating the parenting styles of the original Baltimore families to how the babies behaved in the strange situation, gave some signs of how these things are linked and this is something we will look at more closely in the next chapter, but the key quality, it seems, is responsiveness.

From the very earliest days in a baby's life we have seen signs that how quickly, how sensitively and how much mum reacts to her baby, colours that baby's world. The quality of communication between baby and mum depends very much on how she responds to him – to his cries, smiles, body talk, his 'conversation', jokes – and these responses are not just to do with the hard currency of physical care – the feeding, the keeping warm, the changing – they are to do with emotions.

Plenty of children, especially those in institutions, are well enough cared for physically, but emotionally they are undernourished.

The role played by emotions – a stormy story in psychology's script – takes centre stage in the next chapter when babies, now nine months old, begin to show their full range.

Sweet Goodbyes

Partings, now that babies are beginning to show what psychologists call 'separation anxiety', can be painful affairs. Professor Edward Melhuish gives a few common sense tips to make them easier:

- Do whatever you can to try to ease the strangeness of the situation.
- Try to leave your baby in a familiar environment. If this has to be someone else's home take your baby there beforehand so the place is not strange to them.
- Leave your baby with a familiar person. If you are planning to use a friend as a babysitter take your baby to meet them once or twice before leaving him.
- Favourite and familiar toys left with your baby can act as a source of comfort.

Is it better to tell the baby you are going or better to sneak out when he is not watching?

Professor Melhuish says:

'At this age it really depends on the nature of the child. Babies differ enormously in their reactions. If you have a child who is very sensitive to separations and gets extremely upset it is probably easier all round to slip out when he is not watching. If you do say goodbye it is probably better to keep it short unless the baby is in unfamiliar surroundings. In that case, stay for half an hour to let the child settle in before leaving.'

Fascinating Findings

From the age of about eight months major changes take place in babies which allow their behaviour to become much more flexible. For the first time they are able to share their interest in an object with another person. They begin to show more of their own initiative in relationships where before they tended to be reactive. They begin to give toys as well as to take them, to start games as well as to join them.

Some psychologists, impressed by how predictably babies show a fear of strangers, refer to it as 'eight-month anxiety'.

Babies tend to show distress when mum or dad leave the room — 'separation anxiety' — about a month after they first show fear of strangers.

How fearful babies are does have some genetic component. Studies of identical twins have shown that they are more alike in how they react to strangers than are non-identical twins.

Distress at being separated from mum peaks at around fifteen months then gradually subsides. This is a pattern which seems to be shown by babies in a variety of cultures from Kalahari bushmen to Israeli kibbutzniks.

Researchers have found that babies left with a total stranger cope much better with separation than babies who are left completely alone.

The longer parents take to say goodbye the harder it is for young babies to adjust to being without them.

At twelve months it makes no difference to babies whether parents say 'bye bye' to them or not before going out. But it does help older babies if mum and dad have made some parting gesture.

Children are frightened of different things as they get older. Scary monsters top the league when they are about seven years old, followed by situations concerning personal safety such as 'someone bad getting into my house'. But by about eleven or twelve years old it is school and social relationships that are the focus for most fears.

Babies are not always most closely attached to those feed and care for them physically. In a much-quoted study in Scotland in the 1960s Rudolph Schaffer found it was those who spent 'social time' playing with and talking with babies who won their affections. For some babies in big families where mum's role was primarily as caretaker, the baby's greatest attachment was to the aunts, uncles, brothers and sisters who played with him.

Researchers have found that babies within happy marriages are more likely to be securely attached than those within unhappy marriages.

Do babies who are carried around in slings become more securely attached to their mothers than those kept in baby seats? A study in Columbia gave one group of mothers cloth pouches to carry their babies and another group free-standing infant chairs. At thirteen months both were tested in the 'strange situation'. The sling-raised babies were found to be more securely attached.

What you can do with your baby

The Treasure Basket

A fir cone, a velvet-lined box, a bunch of bells, a spiral-bound notebook, a feather, a bath plug with chain, a lemon... Between six and nine months, when babies have only recently learned to sit up and grasp accurately, the world of things takes on a huge new fascination. Whereas previously they loved nothing better than a bit of live company, now babies love to handle objects, to touch, mouth, feel, explore whatever comes within arms' reach. Imagine at such a stage, plunging your hand into a box of delights. That is the idea behind the treasure basket. This wonderfully simple but stimulating concept has been dreamed up by childcare expert Elinor Goldschmied who sees the treasure basket as one way of enriching the baby's experience at a time when his brain is growing particularly fast.

'Babies who can sit independently but not yet move need a wide variety of different objects to engage their interest and excite their developing senses and understanding,' she says. 'The basket brings together a rich variety of everyday things – things which feel interesting to the five senses: hearing, sight, taste, touch and smell.'

The sense of hearing can be stimulated with rattles of different types, castanets, a triangle, a bamboo whistle, a harmonica. Sight with the many different forms, shapes and colours of things as well as shiny foil and brightly-coloured things like alabaster eggs and woolly balls. Taste is a little harder to cater for, but babies are likely to mouth most of the items and the addition of an apple or a lemon could be interesting for them. Smell can be stimulated with little

*An orange, a zipped purse, a rolling bell — items in the treasure
basket are chosen to stimulate all the senses.*

bags of lavender, peppermint and cloves. And the treasure box is a
particularly rich source of touch. There are so many different
textures, shapes, sizes and forms which can be explored — a tea-
strainer, natural sponge, hairbrush, velvet powder puff, miniature
basket, bunch of keys...Do not include anything that is small
enough to be swallowed or poked into nose or ears. Care must also
be taken that nothing sharp or pointed is included, and the items
should be changed regularly so there are always surprises to engage
the baby's interest.

You do not have to spend a lot of money on what are so-called 'educational' toys to keep babies amused and help their development. The treasure basket, which can capture even a young baby's attention for as long as forty minutes at a time, can be put together for almost nothing. None of its contents are bought toys, nearly all are safe everyday items found in most households.

One rule of the basket, as far as Elinor is concerned, is that items should only be of natural materials – no plastic. In her recent book, *People Under Three*, she explains that the 'sameness' of plastic and the fact that it is so widely used to make children's toys makes it less interesting to touch than many a natural material. She also believes that, while an adult should be on hand as an 'emotional anchor', adults should take a back seat and allow babies to explore the contents of the basket at their own pace and in their own way.

CHAPTER 10

Emotion - A Time to Share

At about nine months a new ingredient creeps, almost unnoticed, into the relationships between babies and their parents. It is subtle and for the most part quite unconscious, but there are signs which hint that it could be something which shapes that baby and her relationships for the future. It is all to do with how feelings are – or are not – shared. By this time babies are capable of showing a wide range of emotions – joy, disgust, excitement, interest, fear, anger and sadness.

Psychoanalysts, like Daniel Stern, argue that how these feelings are handled by those closest to the baby seems to leave its thumbprint on her... sometimes for life. How does it work?

Mum is chatting over coffee to her friend. At her feet, Angela is doing a tummy crawl towards a new rattle. With half an eye on her baby, mum chats on.

Angela gets more excited as she gets close to her goal. Finally she grabs the rattle and bangs it up and down on the floor with great gusto, smiling as she does so.

Broadly there are two styles of parenting – tuning in to what your baby is interested in...

Mum turns, mid-sentence, saying 'Bang, bang, bang' to
Angela and nodding her head up and down in time with each word.

Angela gives no sign that she has even heard. She goes on
with her rattle bashing.

Meanwhile mum has turned back to her companion, picking
up exactly where she left off as if nothing had happened.

...or taking the lead.

If you stop and examine what happened here under the psychological microscope it is an illuminating molecule of the chemistry of their relationship. What mum did was to match Angela's rattle-bashing with her voice and the movement of her head. She matched it in its intensity – by moving her head vigorously; in its timing – a nod for every bang; and in its shape – by moving her head up and down just as Angela had moved the rattle up and down. This was not just mum imitating Angela's movement, she was tuning in to what Angela was feeling and sharing that with the baby.

Ask mum why she did what she did, and if forced to stop and think about it, she is likely to say something like: 'To join in'.

This process is what Stern calls in psycho-jargon 'affect attunement'. According to him this experience of sharing feelings runs like a river through the baby's minute-by-minute experience of life colouring the waters as it goes.

Some babies will find most of their feelings – positive and negative – can be shared and confirmed in another. Others, whose parents are less responsive, will find that some feelings – particularly bad ones – are only experienced alone. Interestingly neither mums nor babies show much sign that they are aware of what is going on. Mothers usually treat this tuning in to their baby's waveband as unworthy of comment, the most natural thing in the world, and babies – like radio stations – give little outward sign that they notice anyone has tuned in at all. So where is the evidence that attunement is actually taking place?

There are two answers to this. First of all observation – by putting under the psychological microscope the behaviour of hundreds of mums and babies playing together the pattern emerges. The second answer comes by watching what happens when the situation goes wrong. What if mum mistunes her radio and the signal she reflects is distorted?

Angela's mother has been asked to get it wrong on purpose — to react as if Angela was a good deal less excited about the rattle than she actually is.

Angela bangs the rattle up and down vigorously — one, two, three, four times.

Mum nods her head in a very lukewarm way with a 'yeah yeah' which is out of time and not at all reflecting Angela's brio.

Angela looks up at once as if to say 'Hey! What's going on?'

Similarly when mum overstates her baby's excitement: Angela gives the rattle the briefest of twitches.

Mum leaps in with a vigorous 'bang, bang, bang!' accompanied by exaggerated moves of her whole body.

The baby looks up quickly at mum's face to check out what is happening.

There are hints from the clinicians' couch that some babies whose mothers often get their attunement wrong, over- or under-estimating how excited their babies are, may give up trying to control their own emotional experiences and become passive or even apathetic, at least in that particular relationship. They become so used to mum setting things at her tempo that they lose the initiative to pace themselves and may even learn to distrust how they feel inside.

This view of babies as soft creatures moulded by their early relationships is not universally held. Other leading figures outside the psychoanalytic field, such as Professor Colwyn Trevarthen, regard babies as much more robust, resilient and active in controlling their interactions.

'I think it is important not to make mothers feel babies are so fragile,' he says. 'We have a lot of evidence that babies are very reactive to the particular individual. If they have a mother who is emotionally very difficult they can be withdrawn with her, but not with the father. That means the baby is not totally dependent on the mother being healthy. We know that when the mother is depressed the baby can be very badly affected. Now some babies may appear to keep a permanent effect of that, but some babies can seem to grow out of those things completely.'

He believes that psychoanalysts underestimate how active babies are in initiating and controlling their interactions with people.

'Psychoanalysts tend to talk about the baby being fairly shapeless and dependent early on, but I think babies are pretty good at controlling their feelings and using them.'

So it seems that these everyday interactions are not just flowing over our baby unnoticed. It looks as if she is not only acutely sensitive to their emotional load, but may also be active in directing it. They sweep her along the course she was travelling, nudging her this way and that, eroding a little bit here perhaps and depositing a bit there while she takes some part in controlling the flow.

To ask how exactly this affect attunement affects her development leads us into the shadowy realms of theory and speculation, but there is plenty of evidence that this is part of the chemistry of the relationship between parents and children. Babies whose parents are very responsive and who share their feelings – bad and good – are more likely to have a secure and strong relationship with that parent.

Broadly it seems there are two different styles of active parenting. No doubt parents adopt a bit of both at different times but, overall, people tend to fall into one general style or another. In one style the parent tends to follow the child, tuning into how she is feeling, what she is looking at, what she is interested in, sharing that and maybe taking it a step further. This is the parent who is reactive or responsive to the baby. The proactive parent is more inclined to take the lead, to set the agenda, to teach and direct and push the child in the direction the parent wants. Taken to an extreme this approach can be described as intrusive – with the parent doing things at cross-purposes to the child at times when she is not ready or open to them.

One of the key areas in which these different styles come out is in how parents handle their baby's bad feelings.

Angela is angry, sad and frustrated. The rattle she so enjoyed has snapped and she can't play with it any more. She is feeling bad and she lets everybody know with her cries long and loud.

Mum sees her distress and comes to the rescue. She picks her up, holds her close and says: 'Poor Angela, you enjoyed that rattle and now it's broken you're feeling bad, aren't you?'

After a couple of minutes Angela stops crying and wriggles as if to say 'Okay let me down now'. Mum obliges, putting her down strategically near a pile of interesting toys.

Meanwhile nine-month-old Nicholas has also met with one of life's little trials. He is sitting by the door with one red Wellington, wailing. He wants to go outside but he is not allowed.

Mum does not try to comfort him with a hug, she leaves him where he is and says 'Don't cry Nicholas. It's really no big deal.'

Nicholas has to control his own distress.

Angela's mother takes the responsive tack, Nicholas's mother takes a directive approach. How will the babies turn out? Put in the bold and simple terms which make psychologists curl their toes – Angela could be expected to develop into a secure child ready to meet new situations and people. Nicholas is more likely to be insecure in his

Grrr. So this is what life's about. Sometimes you feel good… and sometimes you feel like a bear with a sore head.

relationship with his mother with all the ramifications of that. At two he will probably lack self-reliance and show little enthusiasm for problem-solving. At five he will find it hard to make friends at school. At six he will lapse into hopelessness if he imagines he is going to be left by mum.

Of course that is an over-simplification. Many other factors play a part in shaping the baby's development – genes, other figures in the baby's life, major life changes. But it paints the broad picture. According to Mary Ainsworth a responsive mother provides a secure base for a child. If a child knows that her base is steady, dependable and there for her – emotionally as well as physically – she is able to go out and explore the world. If not, her explorations are stunted.

Psychologist Howard Steele, in London, is looking more closely at these two parenting styles.

'Up until about eight or nine months, from the attachment point of view, probably the most crucially important thing for parents is to be able to hold the child close when he needs it, but also to be able to let go when he recovers some equilibrium. That's maybe what makes the biggest difference in styles of care – that ability to hold the baby in a spontaneous, uninhibited way, seemingly unclouded by past conflicts or ambivalence.'

To some mothers this comes easily but others are much more hesitant about picking their children up and cuddling them – whether because of their own past experience, their state of mind or because they believe it might spoil the child. The importance of that physical contact was dramatically demonstrated as long ago as 1958 in what is one of the most widely-quoted experiments in the field of psychology. Harry Harlow took baby monkeys from their mothers shortly after birth and raised them with two surrogate mothers. One was a bare lattice of wire, the other was covered with

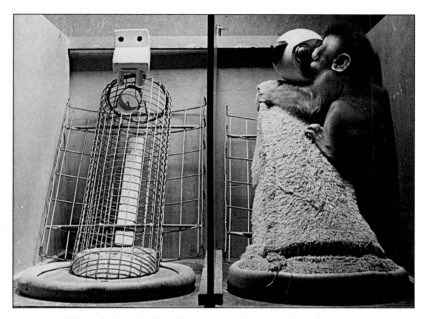

Although he is fed by the wire 'mother', on the left, it is the cuddly one, on the right, that the baby monkey runs to for comfort.

soft terry cloth. Even babies who were only fed by the wire mother preferred the terry cloth mother and spent most of their time cuddling it, using it as a base from which to explore and running to it when frightened. That comforting contact seemed to be far more important to the baby monkeys than any mechanical provider of food.

Once babies are at the nine months stage, however, when they become more active companions, different strategies are brought into play and the varying styles of parents are thrown into sharp relief. A baby's good feelings are relatively straightforward to handle but, according to psychoanalysts, how parents treat bad feelings seems to separate them out.

'Babies learn very quickly,' Steele says, 'and certainly by eight or nine months, they know what parents expect them to do with their bad feelings. In optimal circumstances the nine-month-old is going to be able to express their bad feeling to their mother or father. The parent has transmitted the message: "That's what life is about, feeling good or sometimes feeling bad and knowing that you can turn to me." The parent will have let the child know that they can act as a container for emotions. They will have got a message across to the child saying "Show me when you're upset and I will try to contain it in my mind for a while and transmit it back to you, so you can know that feeling bad is not the end of the world... It will not destroy you, or me, or our relationship. Even when you're feeling like you hate me − as all children sometimes do towards their parents − I can live with that. It's okay, I'm not going to punish you. I'm not going to say that's inappropriate. I'm going to − with you − survive it. And I think what's also important is that I'm not going to take those feelings away from you. I'm going to help you own those feelings."'

The insecure child, on the other hand, has not had that opportunity to share her bad feelings in the same way. Her mother either dismisses what the baby feels: 'Don't cry. It's no big deal,' 'What a fuss to make about nothing,' or she over-reacts to the point where the baby's distress overwhelms her. Gradually the child becomes less and less able to express her pain − walling it up inside or signalling it in a distorted way which is easily misread and leads to more complications. In a strange situation these babies do not run up to mum for hugs and reassurance, they avoid her or they approach her then push her away and refuse to be comforted. As a result their mothers often misinterpret this as rejection. They think 'Look, she doesn't care if I come back or not. She doesn't like me...' and a vicious circle can begin.

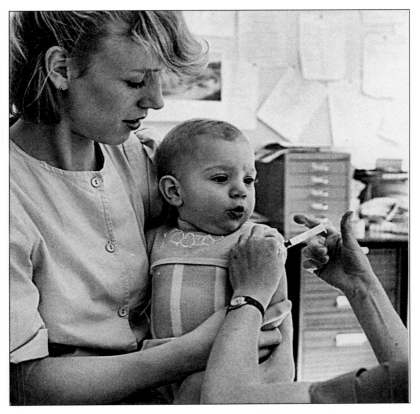

Good feelings are straightforward to handle but according to some psychoanalysts it is how parents treat bad feelings that separates them out.

Putting the psychoanalytical microscope once again over this business of sharing feelings and the ways mothers and fathers interact with their babies, Daniel Stern describes the mechanics of how parents use – and misuse – attunement to shape their baby's behaviour. He talks about parents slipping into their baby's emotional experience and, once there, applying the occasional tweak and nudge to keep it on an acceptable course.

Angela is knocking Hades out of the noisy rattle again.' Yeah, bang, bang, bang,' says mum, drumming her hand up and down. She smiles with Angela 'bang, bang bang'. Then she gives a very gentle up-and-down motion with her hand and whispers 'pat, pat, pat' – her face expectant and 'listening'.

Angela looks at her intently. She, too, looks as if she is listening. She lifts the rattle and pats it down gently.

But sometimes mums can go too far, says Stern. They tune in, then rob their babies of their own emotional experiences.

Kelly loves to bang her wooden doll on the floor. Mum seems to join in with her fun in doing this, smiling and nodding her head in time to the bangs. But once Kelly has taken her aboard her emotional ship, mum pirates it every time. She takes the doll and changes the whole nature and tempo of the experience. She rocks dolly back and forth in her arms with gentle soothing noises – quite a different mood from the dolly-bashing routine Kelly was enjoying.

It's no longer Kelly's show.

Later Kelly is playing quietly with a set of plastic shapes and a post box. Mum interrupts, waving a puzzle in front of her vigorously and casting aside the post box. 'Come on, Kelly, leave those old shapes and have a go at this puzzle for a change.'

Mum is not so much sharing and confirming what Kelly feels but taking over her feelings and her attention and directing them elsewhere – what Stern calls 'emotional theft'. It seems, from his clinician's perspective, that a mother who persistently robs her baby of her experiences could be setting her up for a future flat-broke in emotions.

No doubt parents use a variety of these strategies at different times, but it is the overall pattern they adopt that seems to count in building the relationship with their child.

We have talked so far about two active styles of parenting, but what about the passive parent? What about mothers who are typically unresponsive?

Emotional engineering to tinker with relationships and check out 'what happens if' are ethically tricky. One could hardly justify experiments in which mums were consistently told to ignore their children, or get it wrong, or commit emotional theft, but in one group of mothers – the chronically depressed – these strategies occur 'naturally' quite often. How does it affect the chemistry between them and their babies?

> Rhiannon's eyes sought out her mother's and failed. She uttered a little cry and thrashed her limbs about, but from the sad mother there was no mirrored response. The pattern repeated itself a few times to no avail. The baby flopped, apathetic.
>
> After some time the mother straightened her baby's shoulders with her fingertips, using almost minimal contact. With an uncertain glance she tried to engage Rhiannon's eyes, but the moment had passed. Her baby was unresponsive.
>
> 'I feel sorry for you,' she said, 'sitting in that chair.'

Inappropriate and out of tune... it was the nearest she came to communicating with her child.

Chronically-depressed mothers have a particularly difficult job in relating to their babies – hardly surprising in a condition where the two central features are flatness of emotion and self absorption. Many mothers experience a transient form of 'baby blues', but as many as ten or twelve per cent suffer much more seriously from chronic depression.

Cambridge research psychologist Professor Lynne Murray is one of those who have made this their field of study over recent years. Through the clever use of video techniques she has filmed mothers and their babies in face-to-face communication. It makes a vivid impression to see the nuts-and-bolts of their rapport, gesture by gesture, expression by expression, unfolding on the screen. In this way she can compare the interactions of depressed mothers and their babies with non-depressed mothers and their babies.

The difference can be stunning. The rapport is simply not there. Depressed mothers are noticeably unresponsive to their babies' efforts to initiate a 'conversation'. Like Rhiannon's mother in the example on page 205, they typically miss the cues. When they do react it is often in an intrusive way, breaking into what the baby is doing rather than using her behaviour as a jumping off ground for the next line in the dialogue. They seem to lack the ability to tune in to their baby, and the usual elements of these conversations are often missing or distorted. For instance they often miss out on imitating, commenting on or interpreting the baby's expressions and attempts at conversation in the way that happy mothers do. And they do not talk babytalk.

When you consider that all over the world mums, dads, adults who have never had children and even children themselves lapse into this funny way of talking, unprompted when faced with a baby, it shows the dramatic effects depression can have on the way these sad mums relate to their babies. The flatness of their emotions seems to be carried into the flatness of their voices. Often too, they project on to their child adult-like motives and feelings which seem to stem more from their own state of mind than the baby's. 'I feel sorry for you, sitting there in that chair,' said Rhiannon's mother which seemed to be as close as she could get, to thinking her way into her baby's state of mind. Other typical comments might be: 'He doesn't think much of this old world.'

All in all, the reactions of depressed mothers are more likely to turn off a dialogue rather than to jolly it along. It is no surprise to find that their babies can often be withdrawn, and apathetic – responses which in their turn, do not help foster a happy relationship with mum. The good news, however, is that with a relatively simple screening procedure, mothers at risk from depression can be identified early and, with extra support and training, can be helped towards a better way of communicating with their babies.

One programme in the Netherlands films at-risk mothers – often adolescents who may have had a poor relationship with their own mothers. The videos are taken in their own homes as they talk and play with their babies, then the films are replayed to the mothers taking them through the nuts-and-bolts of the interaction, building on the positives, the things that work.

According to Professor Trevarthen: 'These techniques can help not only distressed mothers who have difficulty meeting their babies' emotional needs, but whole families where trust and intimacy have broken down and interactions are mostly negative. Home-trainers are experts in analysing videos of home life to find the moments when there are successful contacts, when a smile is met by a smile, when space is left for someone else to speak, or when siblings are given a turn. They help families to see and build upon these. With a depressed mother, who may despair of having a happy and responsive baby, video review can show how sensitive the baby is to even the slightest recognition of his or her own signs of need to make contact. And the baby changes so quickly as the mother gains courage and awareness that this gives a strong positive feed-back, pushing their companionship along.'

It is more evidence that babies are emotionally sensitive but not completely fragile; impressionable but not jelly-like; responsive but also active and controlling within relationships... aspects of the developing individual which come to the fore in the next chapter.

Fascinating Findings

Infants recognize emotion in the voice earlier than emotion in the face.

Psychologists talk about 'display rules' for emotion. They refer to the way people hide or exaggerate their real feelings rather than show them in company – for example pretending to like a present that is not wanted. These rules have to be learned by children. As babies they are not very good at hiding their true emotions, but they learn to do so as they get older.

A few babies can stand alone from nine months, some even take their first steps then, but the age range is wide. Some babies do not get going until sixteen or seventeen months, and the average baby stands alone at eleven months and walks at a year.

At around this time (nine months) babies are also beginning to get the hang of the relationships between things. They start putting lids on pots, cups on saucers and spoons in cups. They find this easiest if the things which go together are arranged in a way which makes their relationship obvious – for example if the lid of a pot is left handle-up and near the pot.

Also around this age babies will be starting to spot the similarities between things. At six months if you sit a baby in front of a tray of objects, some of which are identical – say four balls of the same colour, four identical cars and four identical bricks – the baby will pick things at random. By twelve months many babies will pick up three or four identical things in a row before going on to pick up something else. They are beginning to be able to categorize objects.

Children in Britain are getting taller. When they have stopped growing today's boys are three centimetres taller than their fathers' generation and today's girls are 1.8 centimetres taller than their mothers.

What you can do with your baby

Getting To Know You

Adopting a good baby bedside manner is vital for childcare professionals who, because of their jobs, often need to get very close to babies who do not know them. Their advice for making friends with babies is:

• Be sensitive.
• Have the mother or carer present.

Rushing at a baby too quickly can surprise and overload her, and looking her straight in the face can easily upset her. One way to make it easier is to look just past her while talking softly to her mother, giving the baby time and space to handle the new experiences.

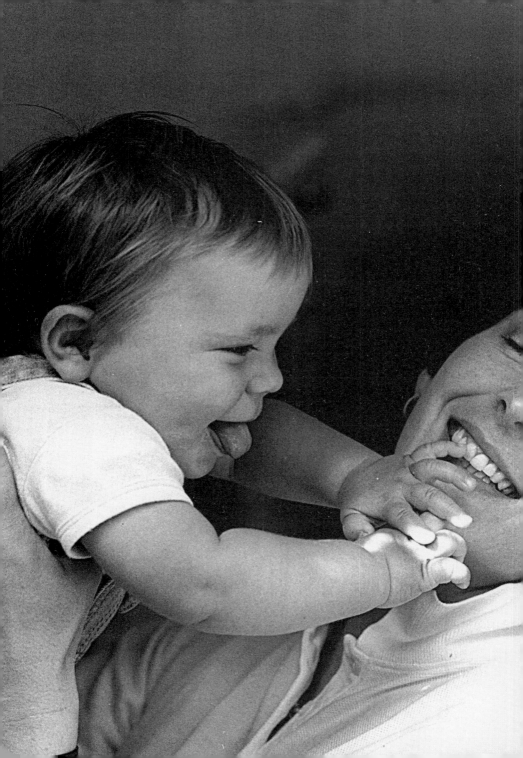

CHAPTER 11

Becoming Aware of other Minds

When babies reach about ten months, one of the nicest discoveries many parents make is that their infants have a sense of humour! Not only do babies laugh at their parents' jokes, they now seem to want to take the stage themselves and amuse others. When parents see junior pull his first funny face or make a grab for the knobs on the television with a cheeky look that says 'I know I'm not supposed to do this', they recognize that the baby is turning a new and delightful corner. Although it has been virtually ignored by scientists and baby books this spontaneous expression of mischief is, in its way, one of the most exciting developments in relationships between parents and babies. It injects in parents a fresh sense of surprise at what might be going on behind their baby's eyes. It is more tangible evidence that he is truly a little character. More than that, they begin to get the impression that they figure in his thoughts.

In chapter five we looked at the baby's sense of himself as a person, and the suggestion from the 'New Psychologists' that babies have some sense of themselves from the start. What about the baby's sense of other people? Does he see mum as a person with thoughts, expectations and feelings like himself? Or does he see her as some kind of super Sindy Doll, but with a more limited wardrobe?

One of the nicest discoveries is to find your baby has a sense of humour.

This is a question which has exercised psychologists for years. Up until recently, the dominant view, pushed by Piaget, and the behaviourists was that babies are self-centred, with no conception of other people's minds until well into their second year. Babies, they said, react to physical cues – facial expressions, hand movements and so on without any notion of the mind operating behind them. Only later do they learn that the person who feeds, comforts and plays with them actually has thoughts in her head too.

This 'behaviourist baby' idea is one of the least popular with the 'New Psychologists' who emphasize how sensitive babies are to emotions, both their own and other people's. They are much more inclined to believe that babies, from a very early age, have an inkling of how people tick. Proving it, of course, is another matter.

The traditionalist approach has been under sporadic fire for a long time, but over the last few years the attackers have come into possession of a number of powerful new guns and it now looks as though the 'behaviourist baby' school is on the run. One of the newest weapons is a battery of baby behaviours only recently brought under the scientific spotlight and referred to in the literature as 'teasing, clowning and mucking about'!

A funny thing happened on the way to the laboratory. Ten- month-old Rhys was helping out with a research project designed round the traditional view – that babies his age have no idea of other people's minds. As the experimenter leaned over him, Rhys grabbed her glasses. She laughed and Rhys offered them to her but, when she stretched out her hand to get them back, Rhys pulled them away, watching her mischievously. She laughed and again Rhys held them out. She reached forward and he snatched them away again at the last moment, laughing uproariously!

It was clear he not only knew what was in the researcher's mind, he knew how to play on it.

An apocryphal tale, perhaps, but one which illustrates the potential myopia of research. Working in an emotionally-charged area like baby development, where parental intuition is rife, psychologists have been so concerned about sticking to the facts over the years that they have tended to marginalize what are often the highlights of baby life - things like fun and high spirits. So seriously have they been studying Rhys and his peers that they have all but overlooked what is staring them in the face – that babies have a great sense of humour! Ask a psychologist what is happening with a ten-month-old and he will talk about cognitive development going through a gear change; he will talk about inter-subjectivity, about object permanence, about separation anxiety...

Ask a parent what stage their baby is at and the chances are they will tell you some story showing the baby's sense of fun – how he laughs when mum pretends to suck his bottle; how he splashes in the bath just to wind dad up; how he falls about at peek-a-boo. It is obvious that these 'comic cuts' are an important part of the baby's behaviour – at least as far as the parents are concerned. Their eyes light up when they talk about the latest mischief their baby has got up to, and many a parental conversation starts with: 'Guess what he did today!'

Until very recently scientists treated this side of the baby's life like an incidental side-show. Look up any psychology textbook and you will find endless references to laterality, to visual perception, memory and categorization in the infant. When it comes to teasing, clowning and mucking about there is virtually no trace. Somehow psychologists never thought the jokey nature of the peek-a-boo player was worth serious study.

That is until 1986 when Vasudevi Reddy, a young lecturer and mother from India, arrived in Portsmouth to take up a teaching post in developmental psychology. Since then her work has thrown a banana skin under the traditionalist position and caused quite a stir in top academic circles. It began, however, modestly enough with a family lunch, a video and a 'Bickiepeg'.

'I had done some filming of my nine-month-old daughter Shamini, for teaching purposes.' Reddy said. 'There was this episode at a lunch – the whole family were round the table and Shamini was in her high chair. She had just learned to offer objects a couple of weeks before and it was a big thing in the life of the family – when she was able to offer something and then release it. There was a 'Bickiepeg' strung on to her chair and she and her dad were offering it to each other, saying 'Ta' and looking pleased. After doing that a few times she called his attention by waggling the biscuit and saying 'Ta'. Then when he put out his hand, she whipped the biscuit back. She was doing this with a half smile... not a full-blown smile but the kind of expression people often call cheeky.'

It seemed that at nine months Shamini knew what was in her dad's mind. She knew he was wanting her to hand over the 'Bickiepeg', and she played with his expectations. It seemed like good ammunition against the 'behaviourist babies' school'.

'Watching this episode much later when I was doing a lecture on pretend play,' Reddy added, 'it occurred to me as very surprising. Pretend-play is a very significant thing in psychological theory. It seems to be the first time infants can hold two images in their mind at one time... and it does not occur in infants before eighteen months. It occurred to me that all this research had been to do with objects – babies pretending that this empty cup is full of milk or pretending that this stick is really a horse. But what was happening here in the video clip was pretending with an action or gesture. The

*Oh no you don't! One of the first forms of teasing is to offer
something then snatch it back.*

child had just learned that holding out an object and waggling it
meant "I'm going to give it to you". And what she was doing was
playing with that newly-learned meaning of the gesture.'

While the traditional approach said social behaviour grew out of
learning about objects – you learn about mum as a feeding station
long before you realize she thinks too – Reddy wondered if
Shamini's antics could be evidence for development working the
other way around. Could it be that babies play with the social
meaning of behaviour first (I'm offering you a 'Bickiepeg'... but I'm
just pretending) and only later extend it to objects (This 'Bickiepeg'
is a plane)?

It was a major switch in thinking and one which fitted nicely with the eagerness of today's psychologists to look at baby development in its social context. The field of teasing was virtually unexplored. A few researchers had paid it fleeting attention over the years, but it had never got much further than an odd mention or two. This was possibly because the first thing academics do when they start taking something like clowning seriously is to define it. You can imagine the discussion: 'Ahem, and what precisely characterizes this infant behaviour, teasing, clowning and, er, mucking about?'

One thing they did agree on was that, like tickling, it takes two. You cannot tease yourself. You cannot surprise yourself with a 'boo' and if you want to surprise someone else you must have an idea about what they are – or are not – expecting in the first place. Now this is what really interested the psychologists – the implications that babies must have an idea of how other people think. They talked about teasing and clowning as 'the alternation of metasignals'. They talked about 'the interactants' attempts to predict and forestall each other'... and there we will leave them talking and go back to Vasudevi Reddy who had persuaded Southampton and Portsmouth Universities to fund her for five months to study babies mucking about.

For the next twenty or so weeks she followed the humorous antics of a dozen babies aged between seven and twelve months, visiting their homes every two or three weeks and hearing from their parents what mischief the little rascals were getting up to.

'That data,' Reddy said, 'gave very detailed descriptions and showed that this kind of teasing – offering a biscuit then whipping it back – was very common. At least half the babies were doing it before twelve months.'

There were other kinds of humour, too:

Rebbeca found that standing up in front of the television when somebody was watching could be quite a game. She would make her way across the room in her baby-walker then stand there giggling and waiting for a reaction. Mum or other members of the family would say 'no' and try to get her to move, but she would stay and giggle until eventually they went into an 'I'm coming to get you' routine and grabbed her away, laughing.

Stephanie had developed a very shrill scream which her parents interpreted as an attention-grabber. In the supermarket her mother would hear her shriek and turn around in alarm to find Stephanie sitting in the trolley grinning at her.

Eleven-month-old Shamini, noticing great grandmother snoring with her mouth open would copy the little round 'o' shape of her mouth – an expression which caused enormous, though slightly embarrassed, hilarity in the rest of the family. Shamini responded to the laughter, looking round at her audience and repeating her 'funny face' with great amusement.

These are familiar events in most baby households but to Reddy's surprise they excited the academic world who had never stopped to look at babies' clowning and teasing in this way. It was a bit like dusting a picture for years then suddenly seeing it as if for the first time and realizing its significance. Here was strong evidence to suggest that, well before they are a year old, babies must, after all, have some idea of how other people think.

The die-hard traditionalists, however, were not going to give up so easily. They maintained that babies like Shamini, Stephanie and Rebecca are really just reacting to physical signals. When Rebecca is standing up in front of the television, they said, she has learned that 'whenever I do this mum chases me'. It does not mean she knows what is in her mother's mind.

Reddy agrees that this is true of some sorts of teasing but not all.

'Sometimes babies tease even when there is no established chasing or tickling game and they do not necessarily go on to develop it into a game. Sometimes you get one-off teases where the child never shows a desire to do the forbidden thing – say touch a hot cooker – though on one occasion the child may try to touch it looking at the mother with a half smile, inching her hand forward.'

There are also different levels of teasing which imply babies know about what people want.

'I'm not saying babies have a conceptual understanding of mind,' Reddy says. 'I'm not saying they have a thing inside their head saying "Ah, this is mind, somebody's intentions, desires, emotions. Hey let's play around with them!"'

What she is suggesting is that babies operate on a psychological level from the start. Instead of splitting the world into the physical and the psychological, she urges fellow psychologists to consider how development might run if these two systems are merged together. Perhaps babies do not have to learn first about actions and then later make a leap to what these things mean. Perhaps that psychological meaning is wrapped up in the action from the start.

This is the kind of philosophy at the heart of the 'New Psychology'. It may not seem a dramatically new idea to parents, but in the hard world of science it is a radically different view of how babies develop. Colwyn Trevarthen, one of the champions of the 'New Psychology', refers to the 'dark ages' of psychological research which have frozen out the very idea that babies might be born with a sense of other people around them and the emotions that go with that.

It has been the preoccupation of researchers to strip behaviour down to its measurable elements and to examine these in isolation – an approach which has made it difficult to study babies in the context of their social world.

It is Trevarthen's suggestion that built into the mind of every newborn baby is what might be called a 'virtual other' – a phantom other person. Babies, then, do not have to learn that other people can feel and think, they grow up with that as the built-in expectation. It is as natural for the baby to see others as people with thoughts and feelings as it is to see Teddy as something soft, silent and sedentary.

Given that babies know something goes on in the minds of other people it is then a small step to ask if and when they deduce what that 'something' might be. Could it be that babies, even quite young babies, might engage in what could be called elementary mind reading?

Their mucking about suggests babies are doing just that. Another situation in which the baby's attempts to 'mind-read' are nicely displayed is in what psychologists refer to in the jargon as 'social referencing'. Again this is one of those everyday events in family life which was only recently 'discovered' by the academics. In the mid-1980s they noticed a pattern of how most babies, from late in their first year, cope with uncertain situations. Since then social referencing has been the focus of many a study. What is it?

Seven-month-old John is getting to grips with a set of nesting beakers on the floor while his mum sits, about ten feet away, with a coffee. Behind the door John's older brother is poised to play a trick on mum and baby. Suddenly a big, black, hairy clockwork spider creeps across the carpet. John does not move. He looks at the spider. He looks quickly and intensely

at his mother. Her face is alive with surprise and fright. He
doesn't hang around to be a hero. Abandoning the beakers he
crawls as fast as he can for mum, wailing in fear as he goes.

Amy is with her mother at a friend's house. She is pushing a
trolley of bricks in front of her when a large white cat ambles
into the room. Amy is not used to cats. She turns at once to
mum who is smiling and pointing to the cat saying: 'Look,
Amy, a pussy-cat. Nice pussy.' Amy takes her cue and, smiling,
sets off with trolley in the direction of the cat.

*Who me? One of those everyday events in family life which can
illuminate so much of what goes on in a baby's mind.*

Thomas is in the kitchen bashing a biscuit tin with a wooden doll while his dad prepares a meal. A stranger calls and comes right into the room. Thomas pauses in his musical pursuits and looks at him uncertainly. Should he be friendly and smile? Should he do a runner for dad's legs? He checks out his dad's expression. Dad doesn't look alarmed... but he doesn't look too enthusiastic either. What should he do? He checks dad's face again for clues. It seems to be neutral. Thomas decides to play it cool and stays where he is, watching.

The way babies read other people's reactions, then act accordingly, is something which becomes noticeable in the last part of their first year. Looking for a lead from someone they imagine knows better than they do how to is also something many adults do in unfamiliar situations. Imagine you are on a visit to a completely foreign culture. You know little about their customs or their laws, their codes of politeness or their taste for hostility. Alone you would be blundering around in the dark learning by your own mistakes... if you lived long enough. But given a minder you keep a close eye on his reactions. If he is friendly in company you put on your best smile. If he is scared you put on your running shoes. It is a short-cut to coping with the world and one which, it seems, babies switch on to very early.

Robots and rubber spiders, white rabbits and scary heads, psychologists have introduced babies to all these to see how they use social referencing. They have even tried to lure babies over the edge of a 'visual cliff' (see page 150) by having mum smile encouragingly on the other side. What the psychologists have found is that social referencing is a very powerful influence on the baby's behaviour.

In a situation where they are not sure how to react, babies take their cues from mum or from dad. If they are not available uncertain babies settle for almost any adult – even strangers – turning to them and trying to read their expressions before making a move. Given the right signals babies may approach the strange and the scary with a smile. On the right word or smile from mum some will even abandon their inhibitions and crawl over the edge of the 'visual cliff'. It is adults' negative reactions that are the most powerful in their effect. Babies may be persuaded against their own judgement to do something they thought might be scary – like stroke a live rabbit – but if the signal from mum or dad is that this rabbit is actually something they should avoid, they pay full attention to the parent's 'negative vibes' and play safe.

The message to parents is to keep their own anxieties in check if they want to reassure their babies in strange situations. An encouraging smile and a clear message that they are happy with what is going on can make all the difference to how their baby copes.

The hints that babies are capable of reading other people's minds – humour and social referencing – start at around ten months old, the time when babies seem to go through a major mental gear change. For the first few months of life babies like nothing better than a live adult for company. Fluffy rabbits, tinkling mobiles, and rattles are simply not in the same league as a living, talking, human being. Then, at about five months old, when junior is getting to grips with all those exciting physical skills like reaching, grasping and holding things his interest switches. Now his preoccupation is with objects - things he can touch and put in his mouth and shake and wave about and explore. He still enjoys live company but on an either/or basis. He cannot talk to dad and concentrate on Fluffy the Rabbit, simultaneously.

Then at about ten months something happens inside that baby skull that allows him to attend to people and things at the same time. Instead of having to choose between dad and Fluffy the

Rabbit he can now share Fluffy with dad and even tell him – in babyspeak of course – about his furry friend. He has reached what some psychologists call the 'joint attention' stage. Mums and dads leap on this chance to chat about Fluffy and all the other things in their baby's world. They are forever pointing out cats and mats, cars and cows, giving the baby a little bit of information about each one: 'Look at the cow! What does it say? The cow says moo'. It is a wonderful time – there is a real feeling of sharing knowledge and feelings and fun. The fact that it is also good for the baby's development seems almost incidental.

The mechanics of this joint attention, at least at first, are sensitively tweaked by mum. Before the baby is aged eight months mums can point as much as they like, but babies will look no further than the end of mum's pointing finger. They cannot follow the pointing signal and they cannot pursue the gaze of another person to see what they are looking at. If mums and dads want to share something which interests their baby it is they who have to make the adjustment. They watch their baby's eyes, see what she is interested in and home in on it... and quite often they do this quite unconsciously.

Gemma is riding on her mum's hip. They are in a waiting room where a long shelf of colourful toys runs all the way along one wall. They don't know it but they are being spied on by a secret camera. The researchers are interested to pick over the fine machinery of this joint attention process.

'Oh look at the donkey,' says mum. 'Isn't he lovely?'

And Gemma is looking at the donkey, leaning forward to get her hands on him. Who saw it first? It is hard to tell.

Mum gets close enough to let Gemma grab a handful of donkey and they discuss donkey things for a moment or two.

'Look at his ears! Aren't they long...'; then 'What does the donkey say? Eee-aww.' She delivers this in an exaggerated voice bubbling with fun and buries her face in Gemma's neck.

They play the game again a few times.

'What does the donkey say? Eeee... ,'

Gemma laughs and contributes the 'aww' on cue, before their attention moves on to the big red fire engine with the bell.

'Oh, look at the fire engine,' says mum and to the casual observer it may seem as if she is directing the baby's attention.

But a closer examination of the timing shows that what is really happening is that Gemma is taking the lead, spontaneously changing her focus of attention, and mum is following it up. She probably does not even realize that is what she is doing.

Mum, having played second-fiddle to donkeys, fire engines et al in these situations for some months, is now finding that she can get in on the act. She can convert what were exclusive infant-object situations into infant-object-mum situations. She monitors very closely what her baby is interested in and she homes in on it, too, but she rarely stops at that. The toy or picture or whatever it is which has attracted the baby becomes the excuse for a little bit of interaction. Mum will point to the donkey, label it, fill in a few details – 'Look at his ears. Aren't they long...' – and perhaps even use it as the starting point for a game 'What does the donkey say? Eeee-aww.'

Gemma, at ten months, is taking part in what, on the face of it, is an unremarkable scenario. It is, however, one of the bricks on which her development is built. Donkey data is coming at her through all channels – eyes, ears, hands – and it is all coming in a social context, via mum.

Sharing an interest in a toy is a good excuse for a chinwag.

There are suggestions that how mum handles this joint attention stage can affect Gemma's development in a variety of ways, as we will see in the next chapter. The trick, according to psychologists, is firstly to follow the baby's agenda rather than impose one on her – to watch what interests her, join in her attention and then tickle her interest a little further – not too much so that she is overwhelmed or left behind, but just enough to keep her interested and reaching forwards.

There is also an emotional side to this. The best learning situations are those in which the teacher is also interested. Surely this is no dry cognitive processing? Surely fun – emotion – is oiling the wheels?

Fascinating Findings

There have been reports from parents of babies laughing as early as five and nine weeks, but generally researchers have found laughing begins at around four months. Even then not all babies start so soon. In one research situation one baby did not laugh at any of the experimenter's 'jokes' until he was a year old.

The development of laughter usually lags behind the development of smiling by about a month.

Just before babies laugh their heart beat slows down dramatically with the slowest beat just before they burst into laughter.

One of the theories behind laughter is that it is a tension reducer. Laughter often follows a very arousing stimulus — something which is unexpected, intense and excites the baby. If that tension continues to mount it can trigger fear and end in tears, but if the tension drops away it is released in laughter.

Watching *Sesame Street* is good for children according to various studies in the United States. They have found that under-fives who regularly watch the television programme improve their thinking skills, including reading, in the process... and the more they watch the greater the improvement. Researchers tested children on tasks such as naming body parts, numbers and letters, sorting, classifying and knowing geometrical forms, before and after six months of *Sesame Street* exposure. All those who watched made some improvements and the group who watched five times a week more, improved the most. After two years of viewing they had wider vocabularies than non-viewers. Later studies have shown that those who benefit most from the programme are the under-fives.

🎲 Babies of under about eight months are unable to follow the direction of a pointing finger with their eyes. They will look at the finger rather than where it is pointing.

🎲 How do babies learn to 'read' adults' minds? Between the ages of three and six months it is estimated that babies will have seen 32,000 examples of facial expressions!

What you can do with your baby

Game For A Laugh?

As jobs go, studying babies laughing must rank alongside compiling a good restaurant guide or quality-testing luxury holidays. What nicer way to spend the day than clowning around trying to coax chuckles out of smiling babies? Curiously it is not a subject which has attracted much serious attention. Researchers have put much more of their time and talents into studying crying. The one big exception is a study at the University of Minnesota in the 1970s which found that what makes babies laugh changes markedly over the first year of life. You may like to try some of their techniques at home.

Alan Sroufe and Jane Piccard Wunsch followed over 150 babies through 300 sessions of rib-tickling, lip-popping and silly walks, to calibrate the infant sense of humour and how it develops between the ages of four months when babies first start to laugh, until they are a year old. They divided their 'jokes' into four categories – auditory, tactile, social and visual.

Auditory jokes included things like lip-popping, talking in a squeaky voice and, the most successful thing at getting a laugh for all ages, saying 'Aaaah'. As everyone knows, it's the way you tell them that counts. The secret of the 'Aaaah' joke is to start off low then build up to a crescendo and cut suddenly!

Tactile jokes included chucking under the chin, bouncing baby on your knee and jiggling him over your head. The best laugh of all, however, came from kissing him on the stomach – just a few pecks would have babies doubled up.

Social jokes were games like peek-a-boo, 'I'm gonna get you', and walking fingers towards the baby.

Visual jokes included sucking the baby's bottle and waddling about like a duck.

Researchers found that babies laugh more as they get older... and they also find more things funny. The youngest babies laughed most at sound-and-tickle games – things like 'Aaaah' and tummy kissing. These jokes, however, were not quite so funny when the babies were older. At seven months the babies showed a dramatic leap in their appreciation of jokes involving people – games like peek-a-boo and 'I'm gonna get you'. Funny looking things, too, like mum shaking her hair about or doing a silly walk also raised more and more laughs as the babies got older.

The suggestion seemed to be that children laughed most at those things closest to the growing edge of their development. So when they are really beginning to show an awareness of other people's minds, they suddenly laugh at social jokes. The unexpected, and the incongruous are funny – but to appreciate the joke you must first have an idea of what is expected and normal.

Nursery Rhymes And Games

These often combine the best of the elements that make babies laugh. Here are a few favourite 'funnies' to try with your baby:

The following is done running your fingers round the baby's palm, then walking them up the arm, and ending up with a tickle.

Round and round the garden
Like a teddy bear,
One step, two step,
Tickly under there!

For the following rhyme, hold the baby's toes between your fingers, one by one, and finish off by running your fingers up the baby's leg.

This little piggy went to market,
This little piggy stayed at home,
This little piggy had roast beef,
This little piggy had none,
And this little piggy went, 'Wee wee wee',
All the way home.

Other nursery rhymes like 'Rock a bye baby' and 'Humpty Dumpty' involve a fall. Building up to the finale, then pretending to let the baby fall is a great source of excited laughter.

Once babies start to enjoy the incongruous, all the world is a stage. Wearing a hat upside down, tying the bib on mum instead of baby, putting a nappy on Teddy, crawling around after babies, pretending to cry for bottles, putting waste-paper baskets on their heads... all these are simple entertainments guaranteed to tickle a ten-month-old's sense of humour.

CHAPTER 12

First Words

There are many milestones in a baby's first year — that first smile, the first time she sits up alone, the first step. All of them are charged with their own excitement and promise, but the most thrilling of all is the first word. It seems incredible that in the time it takes an adult to complete an elementary course in basket-weaving the tiny helpless creature who did not even know how to smile twelve months ago has turned into the one-word wonder toddling round your kitchen and burgling the fridge!

For many this first word will appear around the age of eleven or twelve months, but babies are not strict time-keepers. Some may produce their first word as young as nine months, others may not begin to speak until they are sixteen months. Whenever it happens the effect is magic. Throughout this first year parents and babies have been communicating with looks and smiles, hugs and gestures but the traffic of real words has been strictly one-way. Parents have had to second-guess what is in their baby's mind — like peeping through a misted window on a secret world. The first word opens a door on to that world — maybe by just a tiny chink — but through it can be seen the light beyond.

Books offer some of the richest opportunities for sharing and learning.

Polly's first words are ball, keys, soshie (horse), juice, tractrac (tractor), duck, mama, dada, ta, bye, hiya, more. Lisa's first words are peeboo, hallo, more, no, wannabikit, mornin (in answer to see you in the –?), getcha, Bobo (the dog), car, ball, mumum, hungee.

List a baby's first fifty words and today's psychologists could make an informed guess about that baby's world. They could guess not just where she lives – it does not take a genius to deduce that Polly and Lisa are less likely to be the daughters of nomadic tribesmen than of Western suburb-dwellers – but how they live. Today's linguists are able to make some subtle inferences. By looking at the proportion of words of one kind and comparing them with the proportion of words of another kind they believe they can detect a pattern. It is rough-and-ready, and no one would use it as a rule, but embedded in a baby's early vocabulary are hints about that baby, that mother, and how the two play together – whether they share a keen interest in objects in the world around them, whether they are more into social chit-chat, or indeed whether they do not share much at all. And the link is with what we have seen psychologists earlier refer to as 'joint attention'.

Polly hands mum a spoon, looking at her face as she does so. Mum takes the spoon and puts it in a cup. Polly takes it out of the cup, mouths it and puts it back. These exchanges are what psychologists refer to as joint attention sessions.

Their importance in language development was pin-pointed in 1983 when American researcher Michael Tomasello and his partner Jody Todd at Emory University in Atlanta provided the first direct evidence that they were involved in this area. For six months they regularly filmed a group of mums and babies who had just passed their first birthdays, playing at home with toys. Sometimes in these play sessions the babies were doing their own thing, perhaps running a car up and down or banging two bricks together, while mum was doing something else. At other times the two were obviously engaged in a game or toy together, maybe looking at a picture book or playing with a doll.

Looking very closely at the filmed sessions Tomasello and Todd noted these 'togetherness' sequences of play. What they found was that babies who had spent more time in these joint attention sessions with their mothers had larger vocabularies at the end of that six-month tracking period. It seemed as if these spells when mum and baby get their heads together over something could have a special role in learning language. Why should this be?

Three years later, in 1986, Tomasello and another colleague, Michael Jeffrey Farrar, took these explorations a stage further. They wanted to know what happened in these joint attention sessions that seemed to be so important. To do it they filmed over a score of mums and their babies playing. They then painstakingly analysed the films frame by frame, syllable by syllable, dissecting each interaction. Not surprisingly they found that most of the mums' and babies' conversation took place when they were playing together – actually sharing a toy or game. If they were looking at different things they did not talk so much. However, there was more to it than that.

At these times of joint attention mums spoke in a different way. They used shorter sentences – it was as if they switched into language which would be more readily understood by their baby partners. This certainly tallied, not just with common sense but with a general picture that was building up through research elsewhere. The evidence was that babytalk scorned by one generation of psychologists as likely to confuse babies – was actually geared to making language easier to pick up.

There were also stronger hints that these joint attention sessions were where babies were really learning their words. What was said outside them – according to Tomasello's measurements – did not seem to affect the babies' vocabularies. It looked as if babies were most receptive to new words when they were introduced during those sharing sessions.

To see how this works let us revisit Polly:

> She picks up a doll with interest, turns it over and starts to chew its arm.
>
> Mum says: 'It's a dolly.'
>
> Polly, who is at present immersed in dolly things, is in receptive mode. She is seeing, touching, even tasting dolly. She is likely to add 'dolly' to her vocabulary.
>
> If, on the other hand, Polly is playing with her dolly and mum thrusts a cup in front of her and says: 'Look, Polly, it's a cup!' Polly, whose true attentions are engaged elsewhere, is unlikely to receive, connect and log the word 'cup'.

According to Tomasello: 'At a very young age if your child is engaged in some action or object and you name it, that is easier for them to figure out than if you try to jerk their attention over to what you're interested in.'

It seems, then, that joint attention – particularly where the adult tunes in to what interests the child – could be the hotbed of language propagation. As we saw earlier, this ability to coordinate attention between an object and another person simultaneously is something that babies only begin to acquire in the weeks just before their first birthday. Previous to that Polly could either focus on her doll or on mum, but could not attend to dolly and mum at the same time.

It is probably no coincidence that at around the same time that they can share their attention, babies begin to get the hang of pointing. What better way, when you do not have the words, is there of communicating your interests to other people? Pointing is a hugely effective way of telling others you want the salt, or there is someone at the window, or you like that picture... It is also a skill which, like language, belongs only to humans. Even chimpanzees – the closest animals to man – do not point in the way children do, or share attention in the same way.

Pointing and language go together.

Tomasello who has been comparing chimps and children in Atlanta for some time, is exploring the complex connections between pointing, joint attention and the development of language.

Lisa (eleven months) is sitting in her highchair when she spots an apple on the table beyond. She has no word for apple but that does not stop her communicating. She looks towards dad giving an excited 'dididi' and wriggling in her chair.
'What is it, Button?' he asks distractedly.
She looks at the apple. She looks at dad again.
He is looking at her as he asks 'What is it you want?'
She stretches out her arm, forefinger extended, and points to the apple 'didididi'. Could she make it any clearer?
'Aha... you want the apple. Apple,' he repeats, giving it to her.

It is from everyday interactions like these that, according to Tomasello, babies break into language: 'These mundane interactions – one-year-olds engage in them routinely every day – provide the basis for linguistic reference in which I talk to you about some topic of mutual interest to us both.'

In other words it is a very social thing. Babies learn to crack the language code by interacting with people who speak. It sounds simple, and it is easy to imagine that by hearing it often enough babies just absorb how to speak, but learning language is an immensely complicated task. Sounds and meanings, grammar and syntax - things that children struggle with later in the classroom are somehow produced 'naturally' by the pre-school child. How?

Babies do not become fluent speakers by merely absorbing the sounds of other people talking around them. The children of deaf-and-dumb parents show us that. As babies they may communicate with their parents by looks and gestures but they never hear words from them. Do they pick up language from listening to the radio or television? The answer is no. Learning language is about communicating. It is active and it is sharing.

This is the position now taken by some of today's language theorists who are gaining ground with their interactionist approach. They have moved away from the extreme positions of the earliest linguists, some of whom – the behaviourists – believed that children learned language like rats learn a maze by being rewarded for making the right response. The behaviourists argued that when babies babbled – from the age of about six months – parents rewarded them if they made any sound that was roughly intelligible. Gradually the babies learned, largely through imitation, to pronounce sounds that came nearer and nearer to words and language grew from that. This theory, however, has a number of holes in it. First of all babbling babies do not produce all the sounds of their language and secondly it does not account for the fact that as soon as they start stringing words together babies use language creatively. When Polly says 'soshie juice' as she points to the horse drinking from the trough, she is not imitating something she has heard. She is putting her own words together.

At the other extreme are the 'it's all in the mind' group who believe in a black box in the brain, that meant native speakers had the rules of any language built-in. The most arresting evidence for their theory came from studies of Creole languages. At the turn of the century in Hawaii, sugar-cane plantations were worked by immigrants from a variety of countries – Japan, China, Korea, Portugal. The adults developed a pidgin language to communicate with each other. It took words from the main languages spoken by the plantation workers but there was no common grammar. Sentences could very often be no more than strings of nouns, verbs and adjectives.

What happens to the children of these pidgin speakers? Curiously they do not speak pidgin, they develop a different type of language – Creole. It has a complex grammar and that grammar is similar for all the children whether they grow up in a household that speaks Japanese or Portuguese, Dutch or French. The suggestion is that there is some kind of innate language template which babies can impose. But this did not seem like the whole story either.

Today's thinkers – the interactionists – take the best of both arguments and emphasize the social context in which language is learned. They recognize that people are physiologically specialized for language and that reinforcement has a role, but they stress the dynamic side of learning language and they emphasize the role of mothers and fathers in creating the right kind of experience to allow babies to crack the language code. What is that 'right kind of experience'?

Much of it seems to come naturally to parents. The early face-to-face chats with baby, the way they take turns in cooing and babbling... the use of babytalk for example. One of the questions psychologists asked was: how do babies learn to break down that steady stream of language so that they hear individual chunks of meaning, or words?

Polly is in the kitchen. Mum says to dad: 'I think it's probably about time that we set the table and ate now – I dare say you're pretty hungry.'

It is a long and fairly complex sentence. But when she turns to Polly mum says simply and animatedly: 'Let's have dinner!' All the subsidiary words are automatically knocked out and the stress in her voice is on the one important word 'dinner'.

Through varying their intonation, introducing pauses between words and phrases and simplifying what they say, mothers naturally break down that stream of language into a much more manageable trickle. Gradually babies seem to separate that trickle into smaller and smaller drops.

According to some researchers babies, at the age of about four-to-six months, seem to be able to shake language down into clauses; by about nine months, they have that down to phrases; and within the next couple of months they isolate the individual words. That is not to say, of course, that they do not recognize any individual words before that time. As early as about eight months most babies recognize a small repertoire of words even though they may not be able to produce them.

Relying on mothers' diaries – a favourite method of exploring how babies learn language – one researcher recently found that when they were one year old the babies in his study knew (but could not necessarily say) ten words. In the next couple of months that soared to fifty words, and doubled to a hundred by the time they were sixteen months.

Speaking, on the other hand, lags a few months behind. After hearing their baby say her first word parents often have to wait a painfully long time for the next few to be produced. These first words take the longest to learn – perhaps one-to-three words per month – until the list extends to about ten, then the rate shoots up. The ten-word point varies hugely from baby to baby – it may be reached as early as thirteen months or not until nineteen months, but on average it will be reached around fifteen months.

After that words come tumbling out faster and faster as most babies go through what has been called a 'vocabulary explosion'. It is probably no coincidence that around this time most mothers' diaries cease – they simply cannot keep up with the pace of their babies' language. In the later part of this time babies may pick up a new word every day until the vocabulary reaches about fifty words. Again, the age varies enormously but an average is likely to be around eighteen to nineteen months. About a month or two after that, babies begin to string words together into two-word sentences like 'Mummy juice' and 'bikit allgone'.

Mothers have always believed that babies understand much more than they can say, and the extent to which this is true was recently shown in an imaginative way in the United States by two psychologists, Golinkoff and Hirsh Pasek. With the help of a few scenes from *Sesame Street,* they found that well before babies were able to string two words together they could already understand the implications of having words in a particular order – 'dog bites man' as opposed to 'man bites dog'.

Here is how their method works:

Violet is sitting on her mother's lap between two video screens. There is a loudspeaker between them and above it a spyhole with an eagle-eyed experimenter behind, recording her every glance and how long it lasts. The message comes over the loudspeaker: 'Cookie Monster is tickling Big Bird.' On one screen Violet can see that the Sesame Street character Cookie Monster is indeed tickling Big Bird. On the other screen she sees the situation reversed – Big Bird is tickling Cookie Monster.

Where does Violet look?

She spends more time watching the picture which matches the message.

The researchers would conclude that even though she can only produce single words she understands how word order works.

Over the last few years researchers have looked very closely at those first fifty words in babies' vocabularies to see whether any pattern emerges. Mostly their preoccupation has been with grammar. They have looked at nouns and tenses, prepositions and pronouns, plurals and possessives and asked: 'Do babies learn things in roughly the same order?'

Roger Brown, one of the big names in this area twenty years ago, followed three babies Adam, Eve and Sarah through their development. He found there was a pattern. Among the earliest rules that babies seem to pick up is how to use 'ing' words – these come before past-tense words like 'walked' and 'jumped'. He figured this was because it was easier to latch on to an idea like 'I am jumping' than 'Yesterday I jumped'. Similarly babies – who at this age are often very keen on putting balls in cups and building bricks on blocks – learn how to use the words 'in' and 'on' before they work out 'under' and 'over'. And they are using plurals long before they use 'the' and 'a'. Psychologists explained this in terms of complexity – not surprisingly, babies, they suggested, learn the simplest things first.

A far more interesting thing to come out of studying babies' early vocabularies came from looking at the kind of words listed. What gradually became apparent was a pattern to do with the proportion of labelling words like 'car' and 'bikit' that babies used compared with the proportion of social or expressive words like 'hungee' or 'hiya'.

Different theorists have coined their own terms but the fact that so many have distinguished two groups along roughly similar lines, is in its own way very telling. Put broadly what they suggest is that children get into language through one of two major routes – by learning the names for objects word by word, or by picking up social phrases 'parrot fashion'.

Which route a baby takes may depend on how that baby's mind works — whether she is the sort of person who likes to sort things into categories or whether she is more of a social animal, interested in a rapport. Some researchers have found that babies whose first words include many labels for things tend to be the kind of children who use toys as a way of attracting mum's attention. Or the route taken may depend on mum's style with the baby. Some mothers are more active than others when it comes to translating the world for their babies. Some talk about socks and shoes, about mice and men at every opportunity. They play naming games with parts of the body and picture books. They engage their babies in conversation and tune in to what is attracting their babies' attention. Some put their babies down with a box of toys and let them explore the world their own way. Their baby chats tend to be along the lines of 'hallo', 'say ta', 'here's daddy coming'. These are of course extremes on a continuum. Most mothers do a bit of both and land somewhere in between.

The way these different mothering styles linked with babies' language development was pointed up quite plainly in a research project at the University of Lancaster in 1986. For his PhD thesis, Spaniard Alfredo Brito filmed year-old babies playing with their mothers every month until they were sixteen months old. He put the mums' behaviour under the psychological microscope and divided them into what he called 'markers' or 'non-markers'.

Marking mothers were the kind of mums who talked a lot about pictures and toys with their children. They did not just say 'Look here is a tree'. They would say 'Look the tree has branches, and leaves. How many leaves are on the tree? One, two, three...' They broke down the world and pointed out the relationships between things. They also tended to be more in tune with their babies. They let the children set the course of their play together — whether they looked at a picture book or played with a set of bricks. They elaborated on what their babies were interested in, and all the while they listened to their infants' responses and checked back that they were still interested in what was going on.

Non-markers, on the other hand, were not inclined to break things down in the same way. They might say: 'Look it's a tree. Look here is a bird and there is a house'. They did not elaborate on things to the same extent as the markers and they moved more quickly from one topic to another.

A third group of mothers were classed as 'passive'. They did not interact with their babies much at all in these sessions. Their strategy was to put the babies down with a box of toys and leave them to it.

On indexing the babies' language development the difference in styles was shown in sharp relief. The babies of marking mothers all ranked highest in language measures followed by non-marking mothers, with passive mums taking up the rear.

Why should marking help so much? One explanation is that what the marking mothers are doing is effectively helping their babies to organize and channel their thoughts. 'Look this is a tree. It's got leaves. How many leaves are on the tree?' She is helping her baby see that trees are made up of parts and these parts have names, too. The non-marker simply shows the tree then moves on. The baby will have to do her own tree surgery and analysis. To get a flavour of the difference this approach can make to thinking, psychologists suggest looking at a complex table of figures. How much easier it is to see what it is all about when someone looks at the figures with you, pointing out their relationships.

Could it be that the style taken by mothers actually moulds the way babies think as well as their language?

Other researchers have noted that babies who have the kind of mothers who play a lot of naming games tend to pick up language in this 'word-by-word' way and their vocabularies contain more labels. Babies whose mothers do not go in for these kind of interactions tend to pick up more social phrases at first – like 'Oh dear', 'Bye-bye' – things which are learned in chunks, parrot-fashion. They tend to use language more for expressing feelings than referring to objects. They talk about 'me' and 'you' more, and they are often a bit later in coming out with their first words. They are referred to by some psychologists as 'expressives'.

What happens when you have the kind of parent who imposes their own agenda on the baby – directing her attention this way and that? 'Look at this clown', 'Come and see what I've got', 'Now let's play with this car', 'I've got a good game'.

Tomasello found that mothers who took this directive approach tended to have babies who learned fewer, not more, words for objects. It seems it is not the labelling of things that is the problem – far from it, there is plenty of evidence that can help a child's vocabulary. It is the intrusive way it is done that seems to be counter-productive.

We have talked a lot about labelling things – that seems one of the simplest ways of looking at how babies learn words. But in fact a huge proportion of our language learning cannot be explained this way. How do you label 'find', 'put', 'yesterday', 'the', 'his'? A good deal of language has to be learned 'in the flow'.

Says Tomasello: 'Kids go way beyond watching people point and label. They are much cleverer than that and must do a lot more work than that, making inferences about what we are doing and intending to do. They are working in the flow of interaction as we are taking baths and going places and eating. They're not stopping and having little lessons despite the popular folk model.'

Everyday commands like 'Put on your coat', 'Don't touch', 'Give it to mummy' are, according to some of today's psychologists, much more relevant to children and the way they operate in the world, than any running commentary on the sideshows like 'Look at the bus. See it's a red one and all the people are getting out. There's one with a funny hat...' Children, they suggest, are less interested in description than in the powers of language to communicate intentions – 'Let's go outside', 'Now we'll find daddy', 'Give me the biscuit'. Adults' intentions are something babies have been trying to decode virtually since birth. When mummy comes with a face cloth they learn to expect a wet face. When dad puts his coat on, he is going out. It is out of that kind of experience – guessing what makes adults tick – that babies learn much of their language.

To show just how clever babies are at reading adults, then using this to figure out language, Tomasello set up a finding game for a novel object to which he gave the made-up name 'toma'.

Clinton is looking at a row of five buckets when the nice lady says: 'Let's find the toma.'

He watches as she puts her hand in the first bucket, pulls out a strange plastic thing and puts it back with a scowl.

She does the same at the second bucket, but at the third she pulls out a piece of motor, looks gleeful and hands it to Clinton.

He knows at once that must be the 'toma' and has no difficulty later in naming it. He had worked out what the lady's intention was – 'to find the toma' – and when she had fulfilled it.

In the absence of a point-and-name situation, this reading of intentions gives babies something meaningful on which they can map language. If they cannot figure out what adults are intending to do they have nothing on which they can hitch the words they are hearing. Tomasello explains this to his students with the following example:

'Imagine I am in France and I don't speak French. A woman turns to me on the bus and starts talking – I don't process a single word. But in a train station I do process a certain amount because I have an idea of what goes on – that the man at the counter expects me to buy a ticket and that I will pay and expect some change. The language has something to stick on to. The child is in a similar situation.'

The key, then, to help children learn language is to make your intentions easy to read. One way is through routine games like 'peekaboo' and 'Round and round the garden' where the same things happen again and again and babies learn what to expect – that gives them something on to which they can map language.

As long as psychologists were thinking about language-learning as labelling things they tended to concentrate on nouns. Words like 'car' and 'juice, and 'mummy' were the important things, they thought, in leading children into language. But while studying the speech of his baby daughter, Tomasello began to realize that it was the verbs she learned that seemed to play a key role in leading her from the one-word stage into stringing words together. Locked in each verb is more than just an action like 'put', there is the idea of someone performing the action and someone or something on which it is performed. He explains: 'When I say the word "hit", within it there is the idea of a "hitter" and a thing hit – that is part of the meaning. "Give" has a person giving, a person given to and a thing which is given.'

In other words verbs give a backbone on which to hang language. As children pick them up one by one, they acquire a way of talking about drawing or hitting or giving or eating – who is doing it, what with, what to... Children, says Tomasello, do not have a set of abstract rules that they apply to language, they just have ways of talking about events, ways that they have picked up from adults talking to them as they eat or draw or go to feed the ducks. Once babies crack that language code and start stringing their own words together the door on their minds opens and life's great dialogue moves on to a rich new plain.

We have come a long way with our babies over the last twelve months. Little by little we have seen their minds awaken and their abilities and personalities unfold in delightful and often surprising ways. Helpless they may be at birth but babies, as we have seen, are far from mindless jellies. In that first year they develop at a pace they will never match again in their long journey towards independence, passing milestone after milestone with apparent ease – the first smile, first step, first word...

Babies whose parents use sign language produce their first signs earlier than babies of hearing parents produce their first words.

As their close companions we have shared their excitement and joy at each new discovery, their pain and frustration when things have not gone right, their crankiness, their chuckles and their quiet contented moments. We have seen their personalities blossom in ways we could never have guessed at. Throughout this time we have seen our babies become more and more effective communicators, in looks, gestures, cries, and now on the brink of language. They do not realize it but as they cross that brink, as they move into year two, they are poised to make another fascinating surge in their development – the language explosion. But that is another story and the exciting thing is – this is only the beginning.

Fascinating Findings

🎲   From as early as one month old, babies can tell the difference between sounds such as 'pah' and 'bah' or 'mah' and 'nah'.

🎲   At about two months babies start cooing – making sounds like pigeons 'ooo' or 'coo', mostly when someone is talking to them.

🎲   From about four months they start making single-syllable sounds such as 'ba', 'ga'.

🎲   From about six months they begin to babble – repeating the same sound again and again: 'bababa', 'mamama'.

🎲   From about nine months the babbling gets more complex. It sounds like conversation but it does not have words.

🎲 Babies produce their first words at around a year but by the age of two the average child knows about 900 root words. During peak development from the ages of two-and-a-half to four-and-a-half, children learn, on average, three new words a day. By the age of six their vocabulary has mushroomed to 8000.

🎲 Babbling is not completely random. At least towards the later part it seems to reflect the frequency of the sounds of the native language that the baby is hearing around her. And there is evidence from analysing tapes that babies' earliest efforts to modify the sounds they make to match those they hear are actually inaudible to the adult ear.

🎲 Babies generally tend to learn to pronounce 'b' and 'g' early on. The sounds 's' and 'f' come much later.

🎲 Young babies actually seem to prefer listening to babytalk. An experiment in 1985 by Anne Fernald found that four-month-olds turned their heads to switch on a tape of a woman talking in babytalk rather than the same woman talking normally.

🎲 Congenitally deaf babies begin to babble at the same age as babies with normal hearing – about six months. After a month or two they babble less and their range of sounds is more limited than hearing babies. Psychologists conclude that feedback is important in language development.

🎲 The babies of parents who use sign language often produce their first signs earlier than babies with oral language say their first word. The signers tend to pick up sign words more quickly and are faster at putting words together to make sentences.

In the first half of their first year babies can discriminate far more sounds than they can later. Their sensitivity to tiny discrepancies in speech sounds dulls as they become more familiar with the particular sounds of the language being spoken by those around them. One study found, for example, that English babies of four and six months old could tell the difference between Japanese syllables ki and kii. But by the time they were ten months to a year old they had lost that ability.

A study in the UK in 1986 found that mothers tend to talk more about feelings with their daughters than with their sons. At the age of two, the girls themselves referred more often to how they felt than the boys did.

What you can do with your baby

Giving A Good Start

Exeter University professor of psychology Michael Howe, a prolific author on early learning and genius, believes that input rather than genetics is the key factor in developing children's abilities.

'To a far greater extent than most parents realize, whether a child becomes a capable and intelligent young person depends not just on chance, luck, or genetic inheritance but on the use parents make of early opportunities to learn,' he says. 'It is entirely possible for every parent to provide the kind of early start that maximizes the chances that child will grow up capable, imaginative and intelligent.'

In his recently published book, *Give Your Child a Better Start,*

written along with Harriet Griffey, he identifies a simple code
which parents can follow to help their babies make the best progress
in early learning:

- Do things together.
- Make sure that there are times when your child has all your attention.
- Share your everyday activities with your children – include them
in as much as possible of your daily life.
- Talk *with* your children not *at* them and create plenty of
opportunities when you and your child can respond to one another.
- Never criticize your young child's efforts.
- Be serious about guiding your child towards learning and discovery.

Bibliography

Benson, Janette B., **Season of Birth and Onset of Locomotion: Theoretical and Methodological Implications, Infant Behaviour and Development,** 16, p69–81, 1993.

Bornstein, Marc H., **Information Processing (Habituation) in Infancy and Stability in Cognitive Development, Human Development,** 32, p129–36, 1989.

Bower, T.G.R., **A Primer of Infant Development,** W.H.Freeman, 1977.

Brazelton, T.Berry, **Touchpoints: Your Child's Emotional and Behavioural Development,** Viking, 1992.

Brooks, J. and Lewis, Michael, **Infants Responses to Strangers: Midget, adult and child, Child Development,** 47, p323–32, 1976.

Butterworth, George, **Infant Perception and the Explanation of Intelligence,** The Darwin Lecture, Cambridge February 1993.

Butterworth, George, **Factors in Visual Attention Eliciting Manual Pointing in Human Infancy,** paper presented at a workshop on Comparative Approaches to Cognitive Science, Aix en Provence, July 1992.

Campos, Joseph J. and Berthenthal Bennett I., **The Importance of Self-Produced Locomotion in Infancy, Infant Mental Health Journal,** p160–71, 1984.

Connolly, Kevin and Dalgleish, Mary, **The Emergence of a Tool-Using Skill in Infancy, Developmental Psychology,** 25, p894–912, 1989.

Crouchman, Marion, **The Effects of Babywalkers on Early Locomotor Development, Developmental Medicine and Child Neurology,** 28, p757–61, 1989.

De Casper, A.J. and Fifer, W.P., **Of Human Bonding: Newborns Prefer Their Mothers' Voices,** Science, 208, p1174–76, 1980.

DiLalla et al, **Infant Predictors of Preschool and Adult IQ: A Study of Infant Twins and Their Parents, Developmental Psychology,** 26, p759–69, 1990.

Fogel, Alan, **Infancy: Infant, Family and Society** 2nd Edition, West Publishing, 1991.

Gleason, Jean Berko, (Ed), **The Development of Language 2nd Edition,** Merrill Publishing, 1989.

Goldfield, Eugene C., **Transition from rocking to crawling: Postural constraints on infant movement, Developmental Psychology,** 25, p913–19, 1989.

Goldschmied, Elinor and Jackson, Sonia, **People Under Three: Young Children in Day Care,** Routledge, 1994.

Gunkel, Claudia and Arnold, Mary, **Newborn Perception of Thatcherized Faces,** presented at the International Conference on Infant Studies, Miami, May 1992.

Gunnar, Megan et al, **Effects of Temporal Predictability on the Reactions of 1 year Olds to Potentially Frightening Toys,** Developmental Psychology, 20, p449–58, 1984.

Hetherington, E. Mavis and Parke Ross D., **Child Psychology A Contemporary Viewpoint 4th edition,** McGraw-Hill, 1993.

Hopkins, B, and Westra, T., **Maternal Expectations of Their Infants' Development: Some Cultural Differences, Developmental Medicine and Child Neurology,** 31, p384–90, 1989.

Howe, Michael, **The Origins of Exceptional Abilities,** Blackwell, 1990.

Karen, Robert, **Becoming Attached, The Atlantic Monthly,** February 1990.

Klaus, M.H. and Kennell, J.H., **Maternal-Infant Bonding,** St Louis, MO: Mosby 1976.

Langlois, J.H. et al, **Infant Preferences for Attractive Faces: Rudiments of a Stereotype?, Developmental Psychology,** 23, p363-69, 1987.

Meltzoff, A.N. and Borton, R.W., **Intermodal Matching by Human Neonates, Nature,** 282, p403-4, 1979.

Murray, Lynne and Trevarthen, Colwyn, **The Infant's Role in Mother Infant Communications,** Journal Child Language, 13, p15-29, 1986.

Murray, Lynne, **The Role of Infant Irritability in Postnatal Depression in a Cambridge (UK) Community Population,** in Nugent, J.K., Brazelton, T.B. and Lester, B.M., (Eds), The Cultural Context of Infancy, 3, 1993.

Oates, John, **The Foundations of Child Development,** prepared for the Child Development course team, The Open University, 1993.

Oates, John and Corlett, Linda, **Social Cognition in Infancy Research Project,** Paper presented to the International Psychoanalytic Association Conference, London, March,1993.

Pick, **Motor Development: The Control of Action, Developmental Psychology,** 25, p867-70, 1989.

Reddy, Vasudevi, **Playing with Others' Expectations: Teasing and Mucking About in the First Year,** in Whiten, A., (Ed), Natural Theories of Mind, Blackwells, 1991.

Rosenblith, Judy F., **In The Beginning: Development From Conception to Age Two** 2nd Edition, Sage Publications, 1992.

Sarafino, Edward P. and Armstrong, James W., **Child And Adolescent Development** 2nd Edition, West Publishing Company, 1986.

Slater, Alan and Bremner, Gavin, (Eds), **Infant Development,** Lawrence Erlbaum, 1989.

Slater, Alan et al, **Prediction of Cognitive Performance from Infancy to Early Childhood,** Human Development, 32, p137-47, 1989.

Stern, Daniel, **The Interpersonal World of the Infant,** Basic Books, 1985.

Steele, Howard and Miriam, **Intergenerational Patterns of Attachment, Advances in Personal Relationships,** 5, p93-120, 1994.

Sroufe, Alan and Wunsch, Jane, **The Development of Laughter in the First Year of Life,** Child Development, 43, p1326-44, 1977.

Tomasello, Michael, **Joint Attention as Social Cognition,** Emory Cognition Project Report, October 1993.

Tomasello, Michael, and Farrar, M.J., **Joint Attention and Early Language,** Child Development, 57, p1454-63, 1986.

Trevarthen, Colwyn, **Communication and Cooperation in Early Infancy: a Description of Primary Intersubjectivity,** in Margaret Bullowa (Ed), Before Speech: The Beginning of Interpersonal Communication, Cambridge University Press, 1976.

Trevarthen, Colwyn, **The Primary Motives for Cooperative Understanding,** G. Butterworth and P. Light (Eds), **Social Cognition: Studies of the Development of Understanding,** Harvester Press, p77-109, 1982.

Trevarthen, Colwyn, **Cognitive and Cooperative Motives in Infancy, and How and Why Infants Communicate,** papers delivered to Symposium of Developmental Psychology, Crete 1991.

Vaughn, B.E. et al, **Maternal Characteristics Measured Prenatally are Predictive of Ratings of Temperamental 'Difficulty'** on the Carey Infant Temperament Questionnaire, Developmental Psychology, 23, 152-61, 1987.

Index